A COMPLAINT FREE WORLD

REVISED AND UPDATED

A COMPLAINT FREE WORLD

REVISED AND UPDATED

STOP COMPLAINING, START LIVING

WILL BOWEN

HARMONY

NEW YORK

Originally published in hardcover in the United States by Doubleday Books,
an imprint of the Crown Publishing Group, a division of Penguin Random
House LLC, New York, in 2007.

Library of Congress Cataloging-in-Publication Data
Names: Bowen, Will, author.
Title: A complaint free world : stop complaining, start living / Will Bowen.
Description: Revised and updated edition. | New York : Harmony, [2024] |
    Revised edition of the author's A complaint free world, c2007. | Includes
    bibliographical references. |
Identifiers: LCCN 2023039193 | ISBN 9780593581315 (trade paperback) |
    ISBN 9780593581322 (ebook)
Subjects: LCSH: Criticism, Personal. | Faultfinding. | Self-help techniques. |
    Life skills. | Performance—Psychological aspects.
Classification: LCC BF637.C74 B69 2024 | DDC 158.1—dc23/eng/20230821
LC record available at https://lccn.loc.gov/2023039193

ISBN 978-0-593-58131-5
Ebook ISBN 978-0-593-58132-2

Printed in the United States of America

Cover art by WhiteBarbie/Shutterstock

10 9 8 7 6 5 4 3 2 1

For my daughter, Lia, who is my light, my friend, and my partner in keeping the Complaint Free movement growing and expanding for future generations

CONTENTS

" PURPLE ?! "

PREFACE

Our vision is to get 1 percent of the world's population to take the twenty-one-day Complaint Free challenge. We believe that if we can positively transform the attitudes of just 1 percent of people on Earth, it will have a ripple effect that raises the consciousness of everyone.

As of this writing more than fifteen million people worldwide have donned one of our purple Complaint Free bracelets and taken up the challenge.

The power of calling something into reality by focusing single-mindedly on it was demonstrated in my own life in 2009 as we approached the six-millionth-bracelet milestone. I wanted to present the six millionth bracelet to someone who inspired our movement, someone whose words and example typified Complaint Free living—Dr. Maya Angelou, Presidential Medal of Freedom winner, bestselling author, and mentor to Oprah Winfrey.

When we first began *A Complaint Free World,* we adopted Dr. Angelou's quote "If you don't like something, change it. If you can't change it, change your attitude. Don't complain" as our motto.

The problem was that no one on our team knew Dr. Angelou. I began to do some research and found that many authors and nonprofits had attempted to connect with her with no luck. Speaking to publishers and agents got me nowhere.

At this point we could have given up, or at least begun to consider other options. But we refused to be dissuaded. Rather, I began to tell people that I was going to personally present the six millionth Complaint Free bracelet to Maya Angelou. Many who heard me say this asked, "How do you know her?" To which I responded honestly, "I don't."

"Then how are you going to meet with her to give her the bracelet?"

Again, I spoke the truth: "I have no idea. But it's *going* to happen."

Whenever I had a free moment, I imagined meeting Dr. Angelou. I had seen her on television when she read her poem "On the Pulse of Morning" at President Clinton's 1993 inauguration. I knew she was a mentor to Oprah Winfrey. I knew she was a famous author and educator, but I did not know her, nor did I know anyone who knew her. Nonetheless, whenever people asked how the Complaint Free World movement was progressing, I enthusiastically told them that I was going to present the six millionth purple bracelet to Maya Angelou. Talk about blind faith!

> "Complaining lets a bully know that a victim is in the neighborhood."
>
> —MAYA ANGELOU

At a conference in Kansas City, I bumped into an old friend and told her my intention. She did not inquire as to how I knew Dr. Angelou. She did not ask how I intended to make this happen. Rather, she smiled as she started to walk away and said simply, "Tell her I said hello."

I snapped my head around and nearly shouted, "You know Maya Angelou?"

"I used to book her when she came into town to speak," she said. "I've stayed in touch with her niece."

I then poured out my story of trying to reach Dr. Angelou and how we had hit walls with every attempt.

"I can't promise anything," she said, "but I'll see what I can do."

In a matter of weeks, I not only met Dr. Angelou but I enjoyed a pleasant afternoon with her at her home in Winston-Salem, North Carolina.

How did this happen?

Who cares!

I simply made a decision based solely on faith that seemed far beyond my capacity to realize, and yet because I would not let the idea go, because I saw this as a done deal—a fait accompli—it came to pass.

I not only held the vision of meeting Dr. Angelou and being able to honor her with the six millionth bracelet, I put this energy out into the world by telling other people that this was—not might, *was*—going to happen.

When I met Dr. Angelou we discussed the vision of *A Complaint Free World*. I then asked how she thought the world might be different if 1 percent of the people on Earth kicked the complaining habit.

She replied,

How do I think the world would be, if one percent of the world's population was Complaint Free?

Einstein said, "No genius has ever used more than eighteen percent of the brain." But today's physiologists say no genius has ever used more than ten percent of the brain. The majority of us mumble and get along with five, six, or seven percent.

If we've been able to stay alive at all, alive and future thinking, alive and having enough courage to care for each other, enough courage to love, imagine who we would be if one percent of the world was Complaint Free.

What would happen?

I tell you one thing. I think war would be laughed out of the room. I think the very word . . . war.

If someone said, "War? You mean I'm supposed to kill somebody simply because he doesn't agree with me? Hah! I don't think so!"

Just imagine, people would speak more kindly to each other. Courtesy would be invited back into the living room, and to the bedroom and to the children's room and into the kitchen.

If one percent of our world was Complaint Free, we would care more about the children and realize that every child is our child; the Black one and the white one, the pretty one and the plain one, the Asian and Muslim, the Japanese and the Jewish—everyone is our child.

If we were just one percent Complaint Free, we would stop blaming others for our mistakes and hating them because, in our minds, they caused the mistake.

Just imagine if we laughed more frequently, if we had the unmitigated courage to touch each other; it would be just the beginning of paradise—now.

Presenting Dr. Maya Angelou the six millionth Complaint Free bracelet

INTRODUCTION

If you don't like something, change it.
If you can't change it, change your attitude.
Don't complain.

—MAYA ANGELOU

I n your hands you hold the secret to transforming your life.

It's been over 15 years since I first typed those words, and I am more convinced of their truth today than ever. Over the past decade and a half, more than 15 million people in 106 countries have taken the 21-day Complaint Free challenge and, as a result, transformed their families, their jobs, their churches, their schools, and, most significantly, their own lives.

They have used the simple idea of putting a purple silicone bracelet on their wrist and then switching it from wrist to wrist every time they complained until they completed twenty-one consecutive days without complaining, criticizing, or gossiping. In so doing, they formed a powerful, life-changing new habit. By becoming conscious of and changing their words, they changed their thoughts and began to create their lives by design.

You may wonder how this all got started. I'd like to take credit for it all, but I didn't create the Complaint Free movement, it created me!

In 2006, while minister of a small church in Kansas City, Missouri, I was doing a series on prosperity based on Edwene Gaines's powerful book *The Four Spiritual Laws of Prosperity*. In her book, Gaines makes the point that nearly all people claim to want prosperity, but they spend most of their waking hours complaining about what they already have. In so doing, they repel rather than attract abundance.

Complaining never attracts what you want; it perpetuates what you don't want.

The human desire for increased prosperity is both normal and universal. And when you ask people what they mean by "increased prosperity," the reply is often some variation of "more." They say, "I want more money, more love, more health, more free time," etc. And even as they cry out for "more," people simultaneously complain about what they already have.

As Wayne Dyer put it so profoundly, "If you're not happy with what you have, *why would you want more*?" The first step toward prosperity in all its forms is to be grateful for what you already possess, and you can't complain about what you have and be grateful at the same time.

Since the Complaint Free movement began, a lot has transpired. In addition to more than fifteen million purple bracelets' being distributed worldwide, we have been featured on *The Oprah Winfrey Show*, *ABC World News Tonight*, NBC's *Today* show (twice), CBS's *Sunday Morning*, and National Public Radio.

Stories about the Complaint Free phenomenon have appeared in *Newsweek, Chicken Soup for the Soul, The Wall Street Journal, People, Good Housekeeping*, and other books and periodicals all over the globe.

> "It is always possible to be thankful for what is given rather than to complain about what is not given. One or the other becomes a habit of life."
>
> **—ELISABETH ELLIOT**

Stephen Colbert took shots at us on *The Colbert Report*. Dennis Miller made a joke about not liking the color of our bracelets, a typical Miller tongue-in-cheek jab making a complaint about no-complaint bracelets. On *60 Minutes*, Andy Rooney quipped, "If this guy has his way, I'll be out of a job."

Oprah Winfrey challenged her makeup artist to use one of our bracelets to quit griping. And Oprah's *O* magazine's South Africa edition distributed fifty thousand of our bracelets to its readership.

Twice, the United States Congress has put forth a bill to make the day before Thanksgiving Complaint Free Wednesday as a way to transition from a day without complaining into our national day of gratitude. Plus, dozens of cities large and small have passed resolutions adopting Complaint Free Wednesday in their municipalities.

We created a Complaint Free Schools curriculum that has been used by teachers at thousands of schools around the world to transform students' lives.

Businesses large and small have used our Complaint Free Business program to improve morale, lower turnover, and increase profits even during the economic roller coaster of the last fifteen years.

Churches of every faith have introduced our Complaint Free Churches program to their congregations, resulting in greater happiness and harmony. In fact, I recently had lunch at an Indian restaurant where all of the employees were wearing our Complaint Free bracelets. When I asked my waiter where he got his bracelet, he responded, "Our Hindu temple gave them out."

`I've been hired to keynote conventions around the world, including for banks, insurance companies, credit unions, software firms, direct marketing companies, automobile manufacturers, major accounting firms, national school associations, government agencies, utility companies, and hospitals, speaking to audiences as large as five thousand people.

And as a result of this movement, I've been fortunate enough to see each of my five books become an international bestseller.

People often ask me, "Did you think the Complaint Free idea would become this huge when you began?"

And my honest answer is "No."

I've tried to figure out how I, at that time an obscure Missouri minister in a small church, could inspire a shock wave that resounded around the world, and I believe it's because of two reasons:

1. There is too much complaining in the world.
2. The world is not the way we would like it to be.

And here's the point: The two are correlated. We are so busy focusing on what is wrong in the world, as evidenced by our complaints, that we are perpetuating these problems.

We are obsessed with what is wrong. We complain about anything and everything, and as a result we keep focusing on our problems, which, in turn, expand. Contrary to popular belief, complaining does not lead to solving our problems. Rather, it concretizes our challenges and justifies our inaction in doing anything to improve them.

Since I wrote the first version of this book back in 2008, a lot more research has been done on the negative impact of complaining on our lives and our society.

Inside, we all know the soul-crushing impact of being around a glass-is-half-empty person for extended periods of time, and this was proven by a research project that looked at a group of high school girls.

Researchers identified several girls who met every day at school for lunch, during which their primary mode of communication was complaining. They would complain about their parents, teachers, homework—anything and everything was a fair target for their negative commentary.

"The true nobility comes from being superior to your own previous self."

—W. L. SHELDON

The interesting thing is what happened one day when the girl whom the scientists had identified as the biggest complainer of the bunch was not in school.

What do you think the other girls complained about in her absence? You guessed it—her! They complained the entire lunch period about how negative the absent girl was.

The takeaway here is that even chronic complainers are repelled by too much griping.

Further, this complaining has negative ramifications. In a study published by the American Psychological Association in the journal *Developmental Psychology,* researchers followed a group of 813 third through ninth graders in the Midwest for six months. The students were questioned as to who they considered to be their closest friends and what they discussed most frequently. The results showed that girls who talked excessively to one another about their problems (vented) were more likely to experience symptoms of anxiety or depression. This, in turn, led to more talking about problems and negative feelings, which brought out more venting, which led to more dissatisfaction, which led to still more problems.

Now, before you read any farther, I should offer you a warning. By reading this book, you're going to become more aware of negativity and complaining. In fact, it will be as if someone turned up the volume on complaining in your world. However, once you're aware of it, you can choose whether to participate. And, after reading this book, you probably won't want to.

When I was a boy growing up in South Carolina, nearly everyone smoked cigarettes. I can remember going to the pediatrician to have my asthma checked. Ol' Doc Castles would place a stethoscope on my chest and wheeze as he instructed,

> "The tendency to whining and complaining may be taken as the surest sign symptom of little souls and inferior intellects."
>
> **—LORD JEFFREY**

"Breathe deeply." My doctor wheezed because he would typically have a cigarette dangling from his lips during my visits.

Most people, even doctors treating young boys for asthma, smoked back then. Everyone and everything—people's clothes, hair, breath, homes, furniture, and cars; offices; movie theaters; and more—reeked of cigarette smoke, and yet we were so used to it that we barely noticed. Today, hardly any public place in the United States permits smoking. If you visit a country where people still smoke freely, it's astounding how pungent and noxious the smell of smoke permeating everything can be. And yet the people in those countries, just like people in the United States decades ago, don't recognize the cloying stink of cigarette smoke.

As you move through your Complaint Free journey, you are going to begin to notice how negative most people's attitudes and comments are—including your own! The negativity is already there, you will just become aware of it for perhaps the first time. Right now, complaining is like cigarette odor. It always surrounds you, but you are now going to start to notice it.

And, if you look for it, you may even notice what I call Negativity Chic.

As an example, one of the great things about being a professional speaker is that a lot of events are held in Orlando, which means I get to take my daughter to Walt Disney World a lot. We were there a few months ago and I wanted to buy myself a T-shirt that featured a particular one of the Seven Dwarfs. As we walked through the Magic Kingdom, I went into every gift shop I saw and I found lots of shirts with one, and only one, of the Seven Dwarfs—not the one I wanted. I searched dozens of gift shops in each of the four Disney parks and never found what I was looking for, which was a T-shirt with Happy the dwarf. What I did find was hundreds of shirts, hats, mugs, jackets, sweaters, hoodies, and stickers all proudly sporting Grumpy's face.

This is Negativity Chic. As we left Disney World on our last day I remarked, "Sadly, it seems that even the 'Happiest Place on Earth' has gone Grumpy."

You will really become aware of our penchant for negativity when you watch what passes for "the news."

A couple of years ago, I was invited to speak to the residents of a large but economically challenged city in Canada. The day of my speech, I was invited to lunch with the mayor and other dignitaries from the city, including the publisher of the local newspaper. After lots of discussion about the importance of thinking and speaking positively, the newspaper publisher leaned over to me and whispered sheepishly, "Will, I hate to admit it but if we run a headline that says CRISIS! it will outsell one that reads GREAT NEWS! ten-to-one."

I told the publisher not to feel guilty. He wasn't telling citizens of his city which newspapers to buy. He and other members of the media

"Do everything without complaining."

—PHILIPPIANS 2:14

have just found a way to tap into people's innate negativity bias. Our negativity bias has helped *Homo sapiens* survive as a species because it's safer for us to look for what's wrong, bad, and potentially harmful as a way to avoid threats and potential danger. Unfortunately, as we've evolved, human beings have not shed this negative mental proclivity, causing modern people to be steeped in worry, fear, and anxiety even though we are far safer today than our predecessors.

All media, both traditional and social, capitalize on the negativity bias by giving us larger doses of what's bad rather than what's good, because we have an inherent attraction to negative events.

Ostensibly, the purpose of news is to create a well-informed electorate, the long-held idea being that news educates people as to who best to vote for to create a better society. However, because of what's known as confirmation bias, people are not exposed to opposing views because they only seek out news that confirms their existing point of view.

Negativity bias gets us to seek out bad news, and confirmation bias gets us to only watch news that agrees with our worldview, leaving us caught in an echo chamber of negativity.

I recently listened to a podcast in which an eminent expert

on news and media was interviewed, and he stated that "news is actually just entertainment." And then he went on to define *entertainment* as "that which is shocking and surprising." It's bad news that shocks and surprises us the most, so we just keep watching, listening to, and reading stories about the very worst of humanity.

Bestselling author Esther Hicks said that if the news were an accurate reflection of the day's events, twenty-nine minutes and fifty-nine seconds of a thirty-minute broadcast would be about all the good things that occurred, and the bad news would be just a one-second blip at the end. What we call news is actually bad news. To get the most from your Complaint Free journey, I encourage you to stop watching, listening to, and/or reading the bad news.

Don't worry, if something important happens, someone will tell you. This was proven to me when I was in Mwanza, Tanzania, the day that Michael Jackson died. I went to donate blood early that morning and the manager of the facility ran out to tell me of Jackson's death. Here I was on the other side of the world, and someone made sure that I knew Michael Jackson had passed. So if something significant occurs—especially something negative—other people will ache to tell you about it.

You've got to begin to treat your mind like a garden. In *As a Man Thinketh,* James Allen put it brilliantly:

> *A man's mind may be likened to a garden, which may be intelligently cultivated or allowed to run wild; but whether culti-*

vated or neglected, it must, and will, bring forth. If no useful
seeds are put into it, then an abundance of useless weed seeds
will fall therein, and will continue to produce their kind.

Negative thoughts are seeds we plant in the world through the act of complaining. They will produce. Therefore, guard your thoughts. Protect them. Shield your thoughts from the negativity of others and what people call "news." And begin now to shift your comments from what is destructive to what is constructive.

Never forget that your thoughts create your life, and your words indicate what you are thinking. Keep both your thoughts and your words positive.

Unfortunately, there is a nearly universal misunderstanding as to what positive thinking means.

I was once hired by a trade association to give an after-dinner speech. The attendees at the conference were to have dinner wherever they chose and then reconvene at the event center to hear my presentation.

I was sitting alone at a nearby restaurant when I overheard some of the people from the conference talking to one another in the booth next to mine.

One asked, "Who is the next speaker?"

Rustling through the conference agenda, another responded, "Uh . . . Will Bowen."

"It matters not how strait the gate,
How charged with punishments
   the scroll,
I am the master of my fate,
I am the captain of my soul."

—WILLIAM ERNEST HENLEY

The first person asked, "Will Bowen? Who's that?"

Her companion replied, "I don't know, some positive-thinking guy, I guess."

The way she said *positive thinking* made it sound like a terrible thing, as if the very words tasted bad coming out of her mouth.

Curious, I opened my cell phone and googled the definition of the word *positive*. I was surprised to find that the first definition that comes up when googling the word *positive* simply is "present." Whereas *negative* means "absent."

Positive thinking is always about what is present and what is working, whereas negative thinking (and complaining) is always focused on what is wrong and what is missing.

People confuse positive thinking with being a Pollyanna, as if to speak positively is to say, "Everything will always work out perfectly all the time."

That's not positive thinking. That's ignorant thinking, because things *don't* work out perfectly all the time. To be positive is to take what's present and do the best you can with it rather than to complain and dwell upon what's missing.

This understanding of the true nature of positive thinking negates the concept of "toxic positivity." Toxic positivity ignores the pain and struggle someone is facing by saying pithy things like "Things always work out for the best," whereas true positive thinking acknowledges how difficult the situation is and looks at what can be done in that moment to make things better.

And it all begins with one's own mind. Wise philosophers and teachers have told us this for millennia:

As thou hast believed, so be it done unto thee.

—JESUS, MATTHEW 8:13

The universe is change; our life is what our thoughts make it.

—MARCUS AURELIUS

Our life is shaped by our mind; we become what we think.

—BUDDHA

Change your thoughts and you change your world.

—NORMAN VINCENT PEALE

You are today where your thoughts have brought you; you will be tomorrow where your thoughts take you.

—JAMES ALLEN

We become what we think about.

—EARL NIGHTINGALE

The highest possible stage in moral culture is when we recognize that we ought to control our thoughts.

—CHARLES DARWIN

Why are we Masters of our fate, the captains of our souls? Because we have the power to control our thoughts.

—ALFRED A. MONTAPERT

Remember that your thoughts create your words, and your words shape your reality. Put another way: What you articulate, you demonstrate.

People fall along a great continuum of being positive or negative. Having spoken to tens of thousands of people around the world, I have not yet had one person come up and say to me, "I'm the most negative person you'll ever meet." It seems people have a blind spot as to whether they are optimistic or pessimistic. Their words may reveal this to others, but they don't hear it. They may gripe constantly—prior to my completing the twenty-one-day challenge, I was one of them—but most people, myself included, think they are positive, upbeat, and optimistic.

It is vital that we control our words to consciously create our lives. The Complaint Free bracelet is not a symbol you sport on your wrist to inform others that you support living Complaint Free. It's not a cause bracelet; it's a mindfulness tool that will make you aware of when and how often you complain so you can stop.

When you go through the practice of moving your bracelet from wrist to wrist, over and over, time after time, you will notice your words. In so doing, you will become aware of your thoughts. Your purple bracelet sets a trap for your negativity so it can be caught and, in time, released, never to return.

It is doubtful you can name a life situation that has not been improved by people who have stayed with the process of becoming Complaint Free. Better health, more satisfying relationships, career advancement, feeling more serene and joyous . . . Sound good? It's not only possible but also probable. Consciously striving to reformat your mental hard drive is not easy, but start now and in a short period of time—time that will pass anyway—you can have the life you've always dreamed of having.

This book comes with a FREE official Complaint Free bracelet plus nine Fast Start videos—you just pay shipping and handling for the bracelet. Go to www.ComplaintFree Challenge.com now to order.

1. Put your Complaint Free bracelet on either wrist. You are now on Day 1 of your journey to twenty-one consecutive days.

2. When (not if) you catch yourself complaining, criticizing, gossiping, or being sarcastic, move the bracelet to the other wrist and start again. You're back on Day 1.

3. Stay with it. It typically takes four to eight months to reach twenty-one consecutive days.

Why twenty-one days?

Many believe that it takes approximately twenty-one days of a consistent behavior to form a new habit. Your goal is to make being Complaint Free a habit and your new default setting.

The key is not to get discouraged! If you're honest with yourself, you'll discover that it may take you days, weeks, even months just to get to Day 2. Then you'll complain and be back on Day 1. But it won't take you nearly as long this time to get to Day 2, and your success will begin to compound on itself, making it easier for you to stay with it.

Most people's Complaint Free patterns look like this: Day 1 ... Day 1 ... Day 1 ... 1 ... 1 ... 1 ... 1 ... 1 ... 1 ... 1 ... 1 ... 1 ... 1 ... 1 ... *Day 2!* Back to Day 1 ... Day 1 ... Day 1 ... Day 1 ... Day 2 ... Day 3 ... Day 4 ... Day 1 ... Day 2 ... Day 3 ... Day 4 ... Day 5 ... Day 1, etc.

Some people have told me that they are going to wait until life gets better and then work at becoming Complaint Free. This is ludicrous. Waiting for life to improve before undertaking the twenty-one-day Complaint Free challenge is like waiting until you are in great shape to begin a regimen of diet and exercise.

You want your life to improve? The surest and best tool is a Complaint Free bracelet. Order one at www.Complaint FreeChallenge.com. But don't wait until it arrives. Put a rubber band on your wrist or a coin in your pocket. With every complaint, move the rubber band to the other wrist or switch the coin to another pocket. The point is to do something physical to make yourself aware of your complaints.

Here are some keys to success:

"If you took one-tenth the energy you put into complaining and applied it to solving the problem, you'd be surprised by how well things can work out."

—RANDY PAUSCH

1. Switch your bracelet with every spoken complaint. Some people try to make this more difficult than it should be by switching their bracelet with every negative thought. Human beings think, on average, forty-five thousand thoughts per day, and because of our negativity bias most of our thoughts tend to be negative. But if you keep moving your bracelet with every spoken complaint, your mind will begin to shift over time and seek out what is good and working rather than what's wrong and missing.

2. Always know what day you are on. People who are serious about becoming Complaint Free always know "I'm on Day 1" or "I'm on Day 12." People who fail say things like "I think I'm on Day 8, but I'm not sure." If you don't know what day you're on, you're not taking this seriously.

3. Don't be a bracelet cop. This is not about what other people are or are not doing. If you want to point out another person's complaint and tell that person to switch their bracelet, switch your bracelet first!

Switch your bracelet with *every* complaint. The average person complains fifteen to thirty times a day, so get used to switching that bracelet. It's the act of moving the bracelet every time that furrows deeply into your consciousness, making you aware of your behavior. When you recognize your complaints, you will begin to change.

In this book, you'll learn why people complain, how complaining is destructive to your life, the five reasons people complain, and even how to get others to stop complaining. Most important, you will learn the steps to eradicating this poisonous form of expression from your life.

As I mentioned, more than fifteen million Complaint Free bracelets have been distributed so far. Do I believe that every single person stayed with it until they went twenty-one consecutive days without complaining? No. I'm sure some of the bracelets ended up in a dusty corner of the recipient's drawer.

Diet books are perennial bestsellers because people buy them, try what is recommended for a while, and then, when they discover the diet means they have to put forth effort and practice restraint, give up. They haven't changed their eating habits and soon gain back any weight they lost and more! Then they buy yet another diet book and the cycle continues.

You can read this book and give the whole bracelet thing a try, give up, and then give the next thing a try, or you can stay with this and radically transform your life. The choice is yours.

Let me repeat the words that opened this introduction: In your hands you hold the secret to transforming your life.

Remember that you're now part of a global movement to improve the overall attitude of our world.

> "If I were to say, 'God, why me?' about the bad things, then I should have said, 'God, Why me?' about the good things that happened in my life."
>
> **—ARTHUR ASHE**

And it's working.

If you consider that the average person complains fifteen to thirty times a day—let's say an average of twenty-three complaints per person per day—and fifteen million Complaint Free bracelets have been sent out, even if only *half* of the people stay with it, that's nearly one hundred seventy-three million fewer complaints spoken around the world each and every day. *One hundred seventy-three million!*

Are you excited?

You should be. You're part of a global transformation movement that is improving the lives of everyone.

A COMPLAINT
FREE WORLD

REVISED AND UPDATED

PART 1

UNCONSCIOUS INCOMPETENCE

CHAPTER 1

I COMPLAIN, THEREFORE I AM

Man invented language to satisfy his deep need to complain.

—LILY TOMLIN

Complaining is so woven into the fabric of our communication that it's often difficult to know whether we're complaining. Many times, it's not just what is said but *how* it is said.

A complaint is distinguished from a statement of fact by the energy expressed. "It's hot today" is a statement of fact. A heavy sigh followed by the lament "It's hot today" is a complaint.

In *A New Earth*, Eckhart Tolle explains it this way,

Complaining is not to be confused with informing someone of a mistake or deficiency so that it can be put right. And to refrain from complaining doesn't necessarily mean putting up with bad quality or behavior. There is no ego in telling the waiter your soup is cold and needs to be heated up—if you stick to the facts, which are always neutral. "How dare you serve me cold soup?" That's complaining.

There is negative energy being expressed with a complaint. Most complaints have a "This is unfair!" or "How dare this happen to me!" quality. It's as if the complainer feels attacked by the actions of someone or something and counterattacks with complaints. Complaints are counterattacks for perceived injustices. A statement of fact is a neutral comment intended to inform, rather than harangue or berate, the listener.

You can often distinguish a complaint from a statement of fact by what precedes it. Many complaints begin with something like:

- "Of course!"
- "Wouldn't you know it?"

- "Just my luck!"
- "This always happens to me!"
- "Can you believe it?"
- "No one cares about . . ."
- "Here they go again!"
- "As usual, . . ."

Each of the preceding statements paints the speaker as a victim of whatever situation they are about to comment upon. Whereas facts, being neutral, have no such negative preamble. Facts are simply statements of what is, rather than a negative commentary on the situation.

Complaining about one's lot in life is not a modern phenomenon. Hundreds of years ago, Benjamin Franklin said, "Constant complaint is the poorest sort of pay for all the comforts we enjoy." When Franklin wrote this, there was no electricity, aspirin, penicillin, air-conditioning, indoor plumbing, cars, air travel, smartphones, or many more of the thousands of modern niceties and so-called necessities we now take for granted. Nonetheless, he felt that his contemporaries were far too cavalier about how good they had it.

The interesting thing is that as life gets better, people don't complain less, they tend to complain more! This is because of a psychological principle known as hedonic adaptation. Hedonic, or pleasurable, sensations are nice at first, but over time we adapt

> "Living in a state of gratitude is the gateway to grace."
>
> **—ARIANNA HUFFINGTON**

to them, and they cease to give us pleasure. What was once new and exciting soon becomes just an accepted expectation. The expectation then morphs into an entitlement, and without even realizing it, something we never even had previously becomes something we simply demand without appreciation.

I once heard a comedian talking about being on one of the very first commercial planes to test in-flight Wi-Fi. The passengers on this flight were thrilled to power up their laptops and cell phones to work, read and respond to emails, and watch entertainment while thirty-five thousand feet in the air. Then, midflight, the Wi-Fi crashed and could not be restored, leaving the passengers to complain loudly over having lost something they'd never even experienced before.

Prior to February 2, 2005, when Amazon introduced its Prime membership with free overnight shipping, people in the United States accepted the wait that came with having online purchases delivered or they paid a high premium for getting their packages faster. Then, with the advent of Prime, overnight delivery became an entitlement, meaning that people complain when purchases are not delivered the very next day, or often that same day!

This explains why people in countries with far less money and resources than we enjoy here in the United States tend to be happier than we are—they simply have lower expectations. I saw this firsthand when I led a group of people to Tanzania to help build a children's hospital and we met some of the most joyous people I've ever encountered. The people there are grateful for what they have because they have so little, and they don't walk around with a sense of entitlement. As a result, they rarely if ever complain.

> "What separates privilege from entitlement is gratitude."
>
> —BRENÉ BROWN

A friend of mine's wife lives in a remote village in Cuba. If she's fortunate enough to have electricity, it's only for a few hours a day. Her government turns on the water supply just once each week and she has to scramble to collect as much as she can. She has little food and no air-conditioning to offer her a reprieve from the sweltering island heat. But again, she is far happier than many people in the United States who are driving expensive cars, sipping lattes, and living in large air-conditioned homes, because her expectations are low.

This is not to say you can't enjoy abundance and still be happy. The key is to remember that, because of hedonic adaptation, the more you get, the higher your expectations will become, and the only way to keep yourself from becoming an entitled complainer is to practice gratitude for what you have.

Researchers believe that there are four stages to becoming competent at anything. In becoming a Complaint Free person, you will go through each of these stages, and, sorry, you can't skip steps. You can't race through or jump steps and effect lasting change. Depending on your experience, some of the stages may last longer than others. You might soar through one stage and then become stuck in another stage for a long time, but if you stay with it, switching your bracelet with each expressed complaint, you will master the skill of being a Complaint Free person.

The four stages to competency are:

1. Unconscious Incompetence
2. Conscious Incompetence
3. Conscious Competence
4. Unconscious Competence

Right now, you are in the Unconscious Incompetence stage. You probably don't realize (aren't conscious of) how much you complain (are incompetent). The average person may complain fifteen to thirty times a day, but you probably are not aware of whether you are at the low end of the spectrum, at the high end, or totally off the chart.

A woman drops something heavy on her foot. As the pain shoots up her body, she reflexively shouts, "Ouch!" And this makes sense. It's normal to say "ouch" when we're suddenly hurt.

But many people are an "Ouch!" looking for a hurt. They walk around ouching about the difficulties and problems in their life and then are surprised when more of them show up. If you cry "ouch," the hurt will show up. If you complain, you'll receive more to complain about. It's the Law of Attraction in action. As you complete these stages, as you leave complaining behind, you will no longer be an "ouch" looking for a hurt. You will attract pleasure rather than pain.

In "Ode on a Distant Prospect of Eton College," Thomas Gray gave us the oft-quoted phrase "Ignorance is bliss." As you become a Complaint Free

"When any fit of . . . gloominess, or perversion of mind lays hold upon you, make it a rule not to publish it by complaints."

—SAMUEL JOHNSON

person, you begin in the bliss of ignorance because you are unaware of how often you complain; you then move through the turmoil of awareness and transformation and finally arrive at true bliss.

Unconscious Incompetence is as much a state of being as a stage of competency.

This is where everyone begins their attempt to master any new skill. In Unconscious Incompetence you are pure potential, ready to create great things for yourself. There are exciting new vistas about to be explored. All you have to do is be willing to go through the remaining steps, which will make you a master at living a Complaint Free life and allow you to reap the many attendant rewards.

People sometimes ask me, "Will, are you saying I can't complain *ever*?"

To which I respond, "Of course you can complain." And I say this for two reasons:

One, I'm not here to tell you or anyone else what to do. If I were, I'd be trying to change you, and that means I'm focusing on something about you I don't like. I'd be expressing discontent about you and, by implication, complaining. So, you can do whatever you want. It's your choice.

And two, sometimes it makes sense to complain.

Now, before you feel you've found your loophole in number two above, consider that word *sometimes,* and remember that I and thousands of people around the world have gone twenty-one consecutive days—that's three solid weeks in a row, or 504 back-to-back hours—without complaining at all. No complaints, zero, none, zip! When it comes to complaining, *sometimes* means "not very often at all."

If we are honest with ourselves, life events that justify expressing grief, pain, or discontent are *exceptionally* rare. Certainly there are individuals around the world who are facing very difficult lives, and everyone goes through hard times here and there.

However, many people today are living in the safest, healthiest, and most prosperous time in all of human history. And yet what do they do? They complain!

Little if any of the complaining we do is calculated to improve our situation. It's just a lot of "ear pollution," detrimental to our happiness and well-being.

Check yourself. When you complain (express grief, pain, or discontent), is the cause severe? Are you complaining frequently? Or are you an "ouch" looking for a hurt?

To be a happy person living life by design, you need a very, very high threshold for what leads you to expressing grief, pain, or discontent. The next time you're about to complain about something, ask yourself how your situation stacks up to something that happened to me.

I was sitting in my home office, writing. The house my

family lived in at the time was located at a sharp bend in the road. Drivers had to slow down to take the curve, but just two hundred yards past our house the city road became a county highway and the speed limit jumped from twenty-five miles per hour to fifty-five miles per hour. Because of the curve and the lower speed limit, cars would slow down to a crawl in front of our house and then accelerate rapidly heading out of town. Or they'd race into town and brake quickly just in front of our house to make the curve. If it weren't for that curve, the road in front of our home would have been a very dangerous place.

"Nobody can hurt me without my permission."

—GANDHI

It was a warm spring afternoon and the lace curtains flapped rhythmically in the breeze. Suddenly I heard a sound that snapped me from work: a loud *thud* followed by a scream. The scream was not that of a person but rather an animal. Every animal, just like every person, has a unique voice, and I knew this voice well. It was our long-haired golden retriever, Ginger.

Normally we don't think of dogs screaming. Barking, howling, whimpering, yes, but not screaming. Nonetheless, that's exactly what Ginger was doing. She had been crossing the road in front of our house and a vehicle had hit her. She lay in the road shrieking with pain not twenty feet outside my window. I shouted and ran through the living room and out the front door, followed by my daughter, Lia. Lia was six years old at the time.

As we approached Ginger, we could tell she was badly injured. She was using her front legs to try to stand, but her hind legs did not seem capable of helping. Over and over she yowled in pain. Neighbors poured from their homes to see what was causing the commotion. Lia stood frozen and just kept saying her name, "Ginger . . . Ginger . . . ," as the tears flowed down her cheeks and wet her shirt.

I looked around for the driver who had hit Ginger but saw no one. Then I saw a truck towing a trailer headed away from town, cresting the hill, and accelerating well past fifty-five miles per hour. Even though our dog lay there in agony and my daughter cried piteously, I was consumed with confronting the person who had hit Ginger. "How could anyone do this and just drive off?" I said angrily. "He had to slow down to come around the curve. Surely he saw our dog, he had to know what happened!"

I jumped into my car and fishtailed out of the driveway, leaving a plume of dust and gravel. Sixty, seventy-five, then eighty-three miles per hour along the uneven road, in pursuit of the person who had hit Lia's dog and left without so much as facing us. I was going so fast on the uncertain surface that my car began to feel as if it were floating tenuously above the ground. In that moment, I calmed myself enough to realize that if I were killed while driving, it would be even harder on my family than Ginger's having been hurt. I slowed just enough to control my car as the distance between me and the other driver closed.

Having turned into his driveway and not realizing I was chasing him, the driver stepped casually out of his truck in a torn shirt and dirty jeans. His greasy baseball cap, which sported a profane witticism, was pushed back on his sun-

Hurt people hurt people.

burned forehead. I skidded in behind him and jumped from my car screaming, "You hit my dog!" The man turned and looked at me quizzically as if I had spoken to him in a foreign language.

With the blood raging in my ears, I wasn't sure I heard him correctly when he responded, "I know I hit your dog. What are you going to do about it?"

It took a moment for the shock of his comment to wear off. After regaining my connection with reality, I stammered, "Wh-*what*? What did you say?"

He smiled as if correcting an errant child and then said again, in slow, deliberate words, "I know I hit your dog. What exactly are you going to do about it?"

I went blind with rage. In my mind I saw the image of Lia's slumped shoulders in my rearview mirror as she stood sobbing over Ginger's body writhing in pain.

"Put up your hands!" I yelled.

"What?" he asked, squaring himself before me and grinning sarcastically.

"Put up your hands," I said again. "Defend yourself! I'm going to kill you!"

A few moments ago, reason had kept me from killing myself while driving in a white-hot rage to find this guy. Now his dismissive and cavalier comment about having hurt, possibly mortally wounded, our beloved Ginger had vanquished all reason.

I had never been in a fight in my adult life. I don't believe in fighting. I wasn't sure I knew how to fight. But I wanted to beat this man to death. I was insane with anger. I didn't care if I ended up in prison.

"I ain't gonna fight you," he said. "And if you hit me it's assault, mister."

I stood there dumbfounded, my arms raised, my fists clenched hard as diamonds.

"Fight me!" I demanded.

"No, sir," he said through his remaining teeth. "I ain't gonna do no such thing. And if you hit me, it's assault."

He turned his back and lumbered slowly away. I stood shaking, rage poisoning my blood.

I don't remember driving home. I don't remember lifting Ginger up and taking her to the veterinarian's office. I do remember the way she smelled the last time I held her and the way she whimpered softly as the vet's needle ended her suffering. "How could a person do such a thing?" I asked, choking back bitter tears.

Days later the man's jagged smile still haunted me as I tried to sleep. His "I know I hit your dog. What exactly are you going to do about it?" rang in my ears. I visualized *exactly* what I would have done to him had we fought. In my visions, I was a superhero destroying an evil villain. Sometimes, I imagined I had a baseball bat or other weapon and was hurting him, hurting him badly, hurting him as he had hurt me, Lia, and Ginger.

"Forgiveness is the fragrance that the violet sheds on the heel that has crushed it."

—MARK TWAIN

On the third night of tossing about unable to sleep, I got up and began to write in my journal. After spilling out my grief, pain, and discontent for nearly an hour, I wrote something surprising: "Hurt people hurt people." Taking in my words as if they were from someone else, I said aloud, "What?"

Again, my pen wrote, "Hurt people hurt people." I sat back brooding in my chair and listened to the crickets celebrating the spring night. "Hurt people hurt people? What does that have to do with this guy?"

As I thought more about it, I began to understand. A person who could so easily hurt a treasured family pet must not know the love of companion animals as we do. A person who can drive away while a young child folds into tears could not fully know the love of children. A man who refuses to apologize for spearing a family's heart must have had his heart speared many, many times. This man was the real victim in this story. Truly he had acted as a villain, but it came as a result of the depth of pain within him.

I sat a long time letting this all sink in. Every time I began to feel angry with him and the pain he'd caused, I thought of the pain this man must have lived with on a daily basis. After a while, I noticed my breathing slowing down, my tension easing. I switched off the light, went to bed, and slept soundly.

complain: to express grief, pain, or discontent

During this experience I felt **grief**. Ginger had shown up five years earlier at our house in rural South Carolina. Several stray dogs had appeared at our home over the years, but our dog Gibson always ran them off. For some reason, he let Ginger stay. There was something special about Ginger. We presumed from her demeanor that she had been abused prior to coming to live with us. And, because she especially shied away from me, it was probably a man who had mistreated her. Tentatively, after a year or so, she had begun to trust me. And in the remaining years she had become a true friend. I deeply grieved her passing.

I certainly felt **pain**, real emotional pain that tore at my soul. Those of us with children know that we would rather endure any pain than have our children hurt. And the pain my Lia was going through redoubled my own.

I felt **discontent**. I felt torn about not having thrashed the guy, as well as about having considered acting violently. I felt ashamed for walking away from him and equally ashamed for having chased after him in the first place.

Grief. Pain. Discontent.

When this man hit Ginger, it was appropriate for me to have felt and to have expressed each of these. You may have experienced something equally difficult at some time in your life. Fortunately, such traumatic events are rare. Similarly, complaining (expressing grief, pain, or discontent) should be rare.

But for most people, our complaints are not sourced by such deeply painful experiences. Rather, we're like the character in the Joe Walsh song "Life's Been Good"—we can't complain, but sometimes, in fact many times, we still do. Things are not really bad enough to warrant expressing grief, pain, or discontent, but complaining is our default setting. It's simply habitual; it's simply what we do.

Prior to beginning your trek down the path to becoming a Complaint Free person, you were probably blissfully unaware of how much you complain and the damaging effect of your complaints on your life. For many, griping about the weather, politics, their spouse, their work, their body, their friends, their job, the economy, other drivers, their country, or whatever they are thinking about is something done dozens of times each and every day.

Few realize how often they complain. The words come out of their mouths, so their ears must hear them. But, for some reason, the words don't register as complaints. It seems that complaining is like bad breath—you notice it when it comes out of someone else's mouth but not when it comes from your own.

Chances are you complain a lot more than you think. And now that you've accepted the twenty-one-day challenge to become Complaint Free, you have begun to notice it. As you start moving the bracelet from wrist to wrist, you will realize how much you kvetch (Yiddish for "complain"—I'm not Jewish, but I like the term).

Up until this point, you would probably have said, honestly, that you don't complain, not much anyway. Certainly, you think that you only complain when something is legitimately bothering you. But we often unconsciously overinflate the number and severity of our difficulties in an attempt to make ourselves feel more important.

Why? Because we tend to believe that important people have important problems. So we reason that the more challenges we have, the more important we are. This perspective lowers the threshold of what we believe deserves a complaint.

It's helpful to remember that difficult, challenging, and even painful experiences are a part of life for us all. Complaining about our difficulties does not increase our status, it just creates an echo chamber, sending the negativity back to us.

Everyone who has become a twenty-one-day Complaint Free champion has said to me, "It wasn't easy, but it was worth it." Nothing valuable is ever easy. Simple? Yes. But "easy" is not part of becoming a successful person. I say this not to discourage you but to inspire you. If you find becoming a Complaint Free person (monitoring and changing your words) difficult, it doesn't mean that you can't do it. And it doesn't mean there is something wrong with you. M. H. Alderson put it well: "If at first you don't succeed, you're running about average." If you're complaining, you're right where you're supposed to be. Now you're becoming aware of it and you can begin to erase complaints from your life.

Just switch your purple bracelet with each complaint and start over again on Day 1.

At this point, I would encourage you to take a moment and ask yourself, "Do I want to be a frigate bird or a seagull?"

"Happiness comes when we stop complaining about the troubles we have and offer thanks for all the troubles we don't have."

—THOMAS S. MONSON

As I write this, I'm living in Key Largo, Florida, a tropical paradise where I can wear shorts and sandals year-round. Two of the bird species I see outside my window every day are frigate birds and seagulls.

The frigate is an interesting and majestic bird. Large, black, and sleek, with a six-foot wingspan, a frigate looks like the shadow of a glider plane floating lazily over the bay. The frigate bird lives its entire life in the sky, even sleeping in the air, and yet it rarely moves. Occasionally you may see just the tips of the bird's long slender wings bend up or down ever so slightly, allowing the frigate bird to rise and fall on invisible currents of wind.

The frigate bird rarely lands except to mate. Otherwise, it sails effortlessly across the heavens, rising and falling on streams of air, sensing the atmospheric changes and gliding along with whatever the sky presents. It does not resist, it simply goes with the flow, and as a result expends little energy living quiet, calm, high, and free.

Seagulls, on the other hand, are loud, squawking birds that zip to and fro on their short, stubby wings, fighting the air currents rather than gliding along with them. Seagulls are the garbage collectors of the sea, picking up anything they can find to eat, while also swooping down from time to time to catch small fish near the water's surface.

Seagulls often fight one another for limited resources, whether it's a scrap of food or a spot to rest atop a navigational buoy. And they make a constant racket. Their complaining wail can be heard from hundreds of yards away as they shriek and cry.

The seagull is the opposite of the frigate bird. The seagull struggles to survive, whereas the frigate just soars above it all.

So, which do you want to be? A majestic frigate bird or a complaining gull?

It's your choice.

By the way, you may wonder how the frigate bird gets its food if it never lands. The answer is that the frigate soars along and when it sees a flock of gulls catching some tasty fish, it folds its long, sleek wings against its body, points its sharp beak toward a seagull that's managed to find something yummy, and dives like a missile straight toward the gull. The seagull may make a futile effort to avoid the frigate bird but will ultimately shriek and spit out whatever it's carrying. The frigate bird zips past the fleeing gull to snatch its falling food out of midair.

Seagulls, therefore, not only have to live like scavengers, but they often have to find twice the food they need to survive because they have to give half their catch to dive-bombing frigate birds.

Daily, life presents ever-changing currents just like the sky, sometimes taking you up and other times taking you down. But if you can remain calm and serene riding the streams of life like the frigate bird rather than fighting against them like the complaining seagull, you'll live a much happier and more peaceful life.

> "Excuses and complaints are signs of a dreamless life."
>
> **—BANGAMBIKI HABYARIMANA**

American philosopher, author, and educator Mortimer Adler wrote, "Habits are formed by the repetition of particular acts. They are strengthened by an increase in the number of repeated acts. Habits are also weakened or broken, and contrary habits are formed by the repetition of contrary acts." For most people, complaining is a habit that has been reinforced time and again through repetition. However, if you consciously strive not to complain, in time you will no longer default to this mode of expression.

Not expressing a single complaint may not seem like it would have much of an impact on your life, but it begins to turn the tide of the complaining habit that has defined who you are.

How? Because not complaining begins to rewire your brain.

To be more efficient, your brain builds shortcuts that bridge the gap between what you experience and what you think about a given situation. After repeated similar experiences, when something like what you've gone through happens again, your brain jumps straight to the conclusion without having to expend the energy to process the information received.

Brain researchers put it this way: "Synapses that fire to-gether, wire together." The more often you think about some-thing in a certain way, the more you get locked into this pattern of thinking.

People who complain frequently have cerebral neurons that have built bridges toward processing life in a negative way. It's not their fault. It's just that over time their brains have created fast tracks to this way of thinking.

The good news is that your brain possesses a powerful ability to reshape itself called neuroplasticity, meaning that its very neurons can be reshaped and redirected to build new bridges.

Because the brain can be reformatted over time, even choosing not to utter a single complaint about something that might have triggered you in the past begins to erode the bridge of negativity and starts to create a shortcut toward positivity.

This is why the number one byproduct of taking the twenty-one-day Complaint Free challenge is increased happi-ness.

As you complain less and less, or maybe even find some-thing positive to say about a previously bothersome person or situation, your mind begins to break the pattern of irritability often associated with complaining and you end up with more pleasurable feelings.

Psychologists call this "subjective well-being," but you and I know it as "happiness."

I once received an email from a man who had not reached the twenty-one-day goal even after two years of trying. He wrote, "For some reason, I get to about Day 8 and then I complain and have to start over again on Day 1." Later in the email he added, "What's surprising is that even though I have not

> "So oftentimes it happens that we live our lives in chains, and we never even know we have the key."
>
> **—THE EAGLES**

completed the challenge, I find that I'm much happier." Then, in all caps he asked, "IS IT SUPPOSED TO DO THAT?"

I had to laugh. It's as if becoming happier by taking the twenty-one-day challenge was some sort of side effect I should have disclosed—"WARNING: Taking the Complaint Free challenge may induce happiness."

The good news is that the happiness you'll feel will spread to those around you. Here's another email I received that explains how that works:

Hi,

Like thousands, I have already begun changing my focus. I've been doing this for about a week, and I am now rarely complaining. The remarkable thing about this is how much happier I feel! Not to mention how much happier those around me must be (like my husband!). I have wanted to work on my complaining for a long time and the bracelet campaign has been the impetus for my changing behavior.

The subject of the bracelets and the mission behind

them has come up in MANY conversations, so the mission has a HUGE ripple effect where MANY people are at least thinking about how often they complain and perhaps deciding to behave differently. This movement may have a very far-reaching effect as more and more people hear of the idea. The reach of this mission is far greater than those who actually get the bracelets! Awesome to think about!

JEANNE REILLY
ROCKVILLE, MARYLAND

You have the capacity to become a happier person and to increase the happiness of those around you, but it means making new choices. Unfortunately, many people don't put forth the effort and they remain trapped like the man in this old story:

Two construction workers sit down to eat lunch together. The first worker opens his lunch box and complains, "Yech! A meat loaf sandwich! I *hate* meat loaf sandwiches!"

His friend says nothing.

The following day, the two meet up again for lunch. Again the first man opens his lunch box, looks inside, and, this time more agitated, says, "Another meat loaf sandwich? I hate meat loaf sandwiches!"

As before, his colleague remains silent.

The third day, the two men gather for lunch, and the first

construction worker opens his lunch box, looks inside, and then begins to stomp about shouting, "I've had it!

"Complaining is negative goal setting."

—CLIFF TOWNSEND

Day in and day out it's the same thing! Meat loaf sandwiches every blessed day! I want something else!"

His friend asks, "Why don't you just ask your wife to make you something else?"

With true bewilderment on his face, the first worker snaps, "I make my own lunch!"

You, me, and everyone else—we all make our own lunch.

Over coffee, a friend related a real-life version of this meat loaf sandwich story. He told me that two years previously his company had changed their voicemail system. Rather than punching in codes and directions via the telephone keypad to retrieve voicemails, all the employees would have to do is pick up the receiver and say, "Get messages," then speak commands such as "Replay message" or "Delete message."

"That's what's *supposed* to happen," he told me. "The problem is that sometimes the system doesn't work very well, and if there is any background noise or if we aren't crystal clear in what we say, the system either doesn't respond or does the wrong thing."

He went on to tell me about a woman in the next cubicle who often had trouble retrieving her messages. If she said, "Get messages," and the system didn't respond or did the wrong thing, she would shout, *"Get messages, damn it!"* Of course, the expletive after the command further confounded the automated attendant, ensuring that instead of her messages the woman got a meat loaf sandwich.

"She's yelling at a machine," my friend said with a bemused smile. "And her anger makes the problem worse." After a sip of coffee he added, "Now, here's the really funny part. When they installed the new phone system twenty-four months ago, I realized that the voice recognition feature didn't work well so I went into the settings and changed my phone back to manual input. I touch the keys just like before to get my messages.

"When I heard this woman yelling into her receiver, I told her that her voicemail could be changed back to manual input. She was screeching into her phone, *'Get messages, you worthless piece of crap!'* and without even looking my way she sniped: 'I'm too busy right now, I'll do it later!'"

My friend shook his head. "That was over a year ago," he said. "I've offered a dozen times to help her change it back, and every time she says she's 'too busy.' I told her it takes less than thirty seconds to fix but she keeps refusing my help. She doesn't have time to fix the problem, but she's wasted hours over the last couple of years yelling into the phone.

"Can you imagine?" he continued. "She comes into work *every single day* knowing that she is going to wrestle with the voicemail system. She knows she can fix it in less than a minute and yet does nothing. Astounding!"

Are you tired of meat loaf sandwiches? You're making your own lunch each and every day. Your thoughts create your life and your words indicate what you are thinking. Change what you are saying, your thoughts will change, and your life will improve.

When Jesus said, "Seek and ye shall find," it was a statement of universal principle. What you seek, you will find. When you complain, you are using the incredible power of your mind to seek out things that you profess not to want but that

"If you persuade yourself that you can do a certain thing, provided this thing be possible, you will do it however difficult it may be. If on the contrary you imagine that you cannot do the simplest thing in the world, it is impossible for you to do it, and molehills become for you unscalable mountains."

—ÉMILE COUÉ

you, nonetheless, draw to you time and again. Then, when they show up, you complain about these new things and attract still more of what you don't want. You get caught in the "complaint loop"—a self-fulfilling prophecy of complaint→ negative experience, complaint→ negative experience, complaint→ negative experience, and on and on it goes.

In *The Outsider*, Albert Camus wrote, "Gazing up at the dark sky spangled with its signs and stars, for the first time, I laid my heart open to the benign indifference of the universe."

The Universe is benign indifference. The Universe, or God, or Spirit, or whatever you choose to call it, is benign (kind), but it is also indifferent (it does not care). The Universe doesn't care if you use the power of your thoughts as indicated by your words to attract love, health, happiness, abundance, and peace, or if you invite pain, suffering, misery, loneliness, and poverty. Our thoughts create our lives; our words indicate what we are thinking. When we control our words by eradicating complaining, we create our lives with intention and attract what we desire.

In Chinese, the word *complain* is comprised of two symbols, *hug* and *ego*. The Chinese believe that to complain is to "hug your ego." There is profound wisdom in the pairing of these two characters to indicate the essence of complaining.

The ego referred to here is not the one from the Freudian concept of the three-part psychological makeup of human beings. Rather, it is the concept of the limited human self that feels it is cut off from infinite supply.

When you complain, you hug your ego. You provide aid, comfort, and validation to that strident voice in your head that insists you do not deserve what you desire, that limited self that feels cut off from the abundance of the world. You limit your ability to enjoy affluence.

The word *affluent* means "to be in the abundant flow." There is a cascading river of goodness flowing at all times. When you complain, you divert the course of the flow around you. When you begin to speak only of what you desire, you allow the flow to wash over you, drenching you with all manner of goodness.

When you begin to attempt to eradicate complaining from your life, you have years of this habit pushing you toward failure. It's like being on a jet traveling north at six hundred miles per hour. If the pilot turns the jet westward, you will feel your body straining to the right because you have been moving with great speed in that direction. If the jet stays true to its new course, you will soon settle in and no longer feel the pull of your previous direction.

Similarly, your previous habits will pull you when you attempt to change them. As you stay with your commitment to switch your Complaint Free bracelet, you will feel a strong pull to resort back to your negative ways. Keep going. Each passing moment and each switch of the bracelet will soon become a mighty force to transform your life.

CHAPTER 2

COMPLAINING AND HEALTH

Neurotics complain of their illness,
but they make the most of it, and when it comes to taking it
away from them they will defend it like a lioness her young.
—SIGMUND FREUD

We complain for the same reason we do anything: We perceive a benefit from doing so. I remember vividly the night I discovered the benefits of complaining. I was only thirteen years old and was attending my first dance, a sock hop. If you're too young to remember, sock hops were often held in high school gyms and the kids were required to remove their shoes to protect the gymnasium floors, hence the name *sock hop*. These dances were popular in the United States during the 1950s, but there occurred a resurgence with the 1973 release of the movie *American Graffiti*.

No single physical and emotional change is as impactful and lasting as becoming a teenager. As a thirteen-year-old boy, I discovered for the first time that girls were no longer "gross." Suddenly girls were magnetically alluring and, simultaneously, terrifying. Terrifying as they might have been, they nonetheless occupied my every waking thought and haunted my dreams. Thoughts of baseball, model ships, movies, and comics were all swept aside by an obsession with girls.

I wanted desperately to connect with girls but had no idea how or what I'd do if I did. I felt like the old joke about a dog chasing cars that finally caught one and didn't know what to do with it. I simultaneously craved being close to girls and feared going near them.

The night of the sock hop was a typical hot and humid South Carolina evening. In keeping with the 1950s theme, the girls dressed in poodle skirts, bouffant hairdos, saddle shoes, and bright red lipstick. The boys' costumes consisted primarily of peg-leg jeans turned up at the ankles, white socks, a pack of cigarettes (borrowed from our parents) rolled up in the sleeve of a white T-shirt, penny loafers with pennies in them, and hair slicked back into a DA (ducktail).

As hit songs from the 1950s filled the air, the girls stood giggling on one side of the gym while we guys lounged on metal folding chairs on the opposite side, trying desperately to look cool. We *acted* aloof and in control but were actually panic-stricken by the thought of going over and talking to the girls, even though every strand of our DNA begged us to do so. "Let 'em come to us," we joked. If they did, our male pride would swell, and if not, at least they might think we didn't care.

My best friend at the time was Chip. Chip was tall, a good student, and a great athlete. Of the three, I was, well, tall. Unlike Chip, I was quite chubby. When I was a teen, shopping for clothes meant a trip to the dimly lit basement of Belk's department store to rummage through the selection of "husky" (overweight boys') clothes.

"Who would you be if you dropped your complaints?"

—ALAN COHEN

Because Chip was tall and athletic, several of the girls were eyeing him. I don't know which bothered me more: the girls' obvious attraction to Chip or his unwillingness to act on it. He just sat there, even though we encouraged him to get the dance started by going over and talking to the ponytailed and bobby-socked enchantresses who sat waiting for us to make the first move.

"I'm too shy," Chip said. "I don't know what to say."

"Just go over there; let them do the talking," I said. "You can't just sit here all night."

"*You're* just sitting here," said Chip. "You're Mr. Talkative. Why don't *you* go over and say something to them?"

Drug addicts will often remember the first time they tried what would ultimately become their "drug of choice," the narcotic that would consume and possibly even destroy their lives if they couldn't shake their addiction. With my next sentence, I was about to embark on an addiction to complaining that would last more than thirty years.

I leaned in toward Chip and said, "Even if I went over there, none of them would dance with me. Look at me—I'm too fat. I'm thirteen, and I shot past two hundred pounds a long time ago. I wheeze when I talk. I sweat when I walk."

Noticing the other boys looking at me, I continued, "Chip, you're in great shape. The girls are looking at you, not me." The other guys nodded. "I'm just a funny guy they like to talk to, but they don't want to dance with me. They don't want me . . . and they never will."

At that moment, another good friend walked up from behind and slapped me playfully on the back. "Hey, fat boy!" he said.

Normally, his greeting would have meant nothing. Nearly everyone called me "fat boy." It was a nickname that suited me and one that I'd grown accustomed to. I never took it as an insult. These were my friends, and it didn't matter to them that I was fat. But when I was called "fat boy" after having just given a greatly embellished speech complaining about how overweight I was as an excuse to not ask a girl to dance, the effect on our little circle was palpable.

One of my guys glared at the boy who called me fat and said, "Hey, shut up!"

"Leave him alone!" said another.

"It's not his fault he's fat!" a third interjected.

I gazed around the circle as all my young friends looked back at me with great concern.

After a moment's pause, the voice inside my head shouted, "Play it up!" So I sighed dramatically and slowly looked down. We were all seeking escape routes to take us away from having to face and possibly be rejected by the girls. Chip's was being shy. Mine was being overweight. The combination of my complaining about being fat coupled with the timing of a playful insult from one of my friends not only had gotten me off the hook, but also had gotten me attention and sympathy.

> "God created the world in six days. On the seventh day, he rested. On the eighth day, he started getting complaints. And it hasn't stopped since."
>
> **—JAMES SCOTT BELL**

I had complained, and in so doing I had excused myself from doing something that frightened me, *and* I had also received attention, support, and validation. My drug had kicked in. I had found my addiction. Complaining could get me high.

Years later, when another friend and I applied for two jobs at a restaurant and my friend got the better shift, I told myself and others it was because I was fat. "Oh, that's not true, you're great!" I enjoyed being told. When I got a traffic ticket, I said it was because I was fat and people clucked their tongues in contempt at the police officer. It would take me another five and a half years to shed this pet excuse, as well as the one hundred extra pounds that were damaging my health.

In "Complaints and Complaining: Functions, Antecedents, and Consequences," published in *Psychological Bulletin,* psychologist Robin Kowalski writes, "Many complaints involve attempts to elicit particular interpersonal reactions from others, such as sympathy or approval. For example, people may complain about their health, not because they actually feel sick but because the *sick role* allows them to achieve secondary gains such as sympathy from others or the avoidance of aversive events."

By complaining and playing the "fat" card, I had gotten sympathy and approval, and I had expressed a justifiable reason for not talking to the girls. My complaining had benefited me.

Chances are you have done something similar. You may have complained about your health to get sympathy or attention, and/or to avoid stepping up to do something you were afraid of doing. The problem with complaining about our health is that it tends to draw to us the actual experience of sickness. What goes into your mouth determines the size and shape of your body. What comes out of your mouth determines your reality.

Poor health is one of the most common complaints people voice. People complain about their health to play the sick role to get attention and sympathy and to avoid the effort of living a healthier lifestyle. Certainly there are some who complain who actually have poor health, but even this keeps their focus on their struggles, making those struggles more prevalent in their lives.

People who complain about their pain are not only notifying the world as to their suffering but also reminding their own bodies to look for and experience pain.

People often say to me, "Oh, so you're saying I should fake it till I make it."

No.

There is no such thing as "fake it till you make it." As pithy as this trite little rhyme is, it is not applicable to personal transformation. As soon as you begin acting like the person you wish to become, you *are* that person. The first step to being different is to act like the person you

"If you keep saying things are going to be bad, you have a chance of being a prophet."

—ISAAC BASHEVIS SINGER

aspire to become. It is the first step toward self-mastery. To trivialize this most important of actions by calling it "faking it" misses the point.

You're not faking it. You are *being* it, even if only momentarily, and you can build on that effort to begin to change your mindset and, as a result, your health.

Ask yourself, "Have I ever played the sick role? Am I doing it now?" When you complain about your health, you may receive sympathy and attention, but the price you pay is perpetuating your misery.

You have probably heard of someone experiencing psychosomatic illness. When people hear the term *psychosomatic* they tend to think of a neurotic sick person whose illness has no physiological basis.

Psychosomatic comes from *psyche,* meaning "mind," and *soma,* meaning "body." Therefore, *psychosomatic* literally means "mind/body." We are all psychosomatic because we are all a unified expression of our minds and our bodies.

According to Dr. Robin Kowalski, medical doctors estimate that nearly two-thirds of their time is spent treating patients whose illnesses have psychological origins.

Think about that. *Two-thirds* of most illnesses originate in or are made worse by our minds. What the mind believes, the body manifests. Dozens of research studies have shown that what a person believes about their health leads to that belief's becoming real.

A recent story on National Public Radio detailed a study wherein doctors found that if they told patients a particular drug held great promise in curing them, the drug had a far more beneficial effect than it did on patients who received the same drug without such a suggestion. The story went on to report that Alzheimer's patients who had other medical issues such as high blood pressure did not get the full benefit of the drugs they took because, due to their diminished memory, they could not remember taking their daily medications. The mind has a powerful effect on the body.

Back when I was still a church minister, I was asked to visit a woman I'll call Jane who was in the hospital. Before I entered Jane's room, I stopped at the nurses' station to ask the doctor about Jane's condition.

"She's fine," said the doctor. "She's had a stroke, but she'll recover fully."

I knocked at Jane's door, and a weak, halting voice responded, "Who is it?"

"Jane?" I said. "It's Will Bowen."

Entering Jane's room, I questioned the doctor's report. Jane looked to be anything but "fine." She repeated, "Who is it?"

"It's Will Bowen," I said warmly.

"Oh, thank God you're here," she replied. "I'm dying."

"You're *what*?" I asked.

"I'm dying. I've only got a few days. I'm glad you're here, so we can plan my funeral."

At that moment the doctor entered to check on Jane and I pulled her aside. "I thought you said she was going to be okay," I said.

"She is," said the doctor.

"But she just told me she's dying," I said.

Rolling her eyes in exasperation, the doctor walked over to stand next to Jane's bed. "Jane? Jane!" she said.

Jane slowly opened her eyes.

"You've had a stroke, hon, you're not dying," said the doctor. "You're going to be okay. Just a few more days here in Intensive Care and we'll move you into Rehab. You'll be home with your cat, Zorro, in no time, okay?"

A weak smile crossed Jane's face. "Okay," she whispered.

After the doctor left the room, Jane turned her gaze toward me and said, "Will, can you get a pen and a piece of paper, please?"

"What for?" I asked.

"We've got to plan my funeral," she said. "I'm dying."

"But you're not dying!" I protested. "I'll make notes, and when you die—a long time from now—then I can do your funeral."

Jane slowly shook her head. "I'm dying now." And she proceeded to detail her wishes for her memorial service.

On my way out, I talked to the doctor again. "She's convinced she's dying," I said.

She gave a weary smile. "Look, we're all going to die someday, even Jane. But she's only had a stroke, and it's not going to kill her. She's going to recover fully with no lingering after-effects."

Not so. Jane's point of view was so strong that two weeks later she died, and I used the notes I had taken that day in the hospital to officiate at her funeral.

It didn't matter what her doctor said; Jane was convinced that she was dying, and her body believed her and responded to that belief.

When you complain about your health, you are expressing negative statements that your body hears. Your complaints about your health register in your mind. Your mind (psyche) directs the energy in your body (soma) in the direction of your complaints.

"But I really am sick," you say. And you may be.

Remember that doctors estimate that 67 percent of illnesses are a result of "thinking sick." Our minds create our world, and our words indicate what we are thinking. Complaining about an illness will neither shorten its duration nor lessen its severity. In fact, it will often have the opposite effect.

I invite you to consider how often complaining about illness might be an unconscious attempt to get sympathy and attention or to avoid doing something. When you complain about your health, remember that you might be trying to put out a fire with gasoline. You might want to get healthy, but when you complain about your illness you are sending health-limiting waves of energy throughout your body.

"The truly patient man neither complains of his hard lot nor desires to be pitied by others."

—ST. FRANCIS DE SALES

In 1999, a good friend of mine named Hal, who was thirty-four at the time, was diagnosed with stage-four lung cancer. The doctors gave him less than six months to live.

Through it all Hal kept his great sense of humor. One day I invited him to take a walk outdoors but because he was so weak, he only managed a dozen or so steps. We stood in front of his home savoring the fresh air and chatted.

"How do you manage not to complain with all you're going through?" I asked.

Hal smiled and replied, "Easy. Today isn't the fifteenth."

"What the heck does today not being the fifteenth have to do with anything?" I asked.

Hal looked deep into my eyes and said, "When I was diagnosed, I knew it was going to be tough and that I could go through this complaining and cursing God, science, and everyone else. Or I could focus on the good things in my life. So, I decided to give myself one unhappy day each month to complain. I randomly picked the fifteenth. Whenever anything happens that I might want to complain about, I tell myself that I have to wait until the fifteenth."

"Does that work?" I asked.

"Pretty well," he said.

"But don't you get really down on the fifteenth of each month?" I asked.

"Not really," he replied. "By the time the fifteenth gets here, I've usually forgotten what it was I was going to complain about. I choose to be grateful and count my blessings rather than complain about my illness."

Scientific research proves that Hal's approach can work for us all. A study done at the University of California, Davis, found that people who strove to cultivate an attitude of gratitude lowered the cortisol (stress hormone) levels in their bloodstream an average of 23 percent! As a result, their mood improved and they enjoyed more energy, better health, and substantially less anxiety.

Another healthy choice Hal made was to surround himself with upbeat, positive people who talked about health rather than sickness. As a result, he lived two full years longer than predicted, exceeding the doctor's expectations by 400 percent and staying happy and fulfilled all the while.

A study published in the *Archives of General Psychiatry* found that optimists live longer than pessimists, with a 23 percent lower risk of dying from heart failure and a whopping 55 percent lower risk of dying from all causes.

Not complaining and being around Complaint Free people not only improves your physical health but also has measurable benefits to your mental health.

A 1996 study at Stanford University used magnetic resonance imaging (MRI) scans to study the effects of complaining on people's brains. Researchers found that just thirty minutes of complaining, or even just listening to someone else complain, begins to shrink the hippocampus region of the brain, leading to decreased mental function, worsened memory, and a lower ability to learn.

> "Complaining is one thing Eeyores are not afraid to do. They grudgingly carry their thimbles to the Fountain of Life, then mumble and grumble that they weren't given enough."
>
> **—BENJAMIN HOFF**

In other words, complaining makes you stupid!

If you want to live a long, healthy, happy, and smarter life, one of the best things you can do is to stay with the twenty-one-day Complaint Free challenge until not complaining becomes habitual for you.

PART 2

CONSCIOUS INCOMPETENCE

CHAPTER 3

COMPLAINING AND RELATIONSHIPS

It is better to have less thunder in the
mouth and more lightning in the hand.
—APACHE SAYING

Moving into the Conscious Incompetence stage means becoming uncomfortably aware of just how often you complain. You begin to catch yourself complaining but only *after* the fact, and you can't seem to stop. You repeatedly switch your bracelet, but your complaints don't seem to be diminishing. I've heard some refer to this as the "Stop me before I complain again" stage.

Sadly, many people give up at this point. For the first time, they are so conscious of how often they gripe, and their incompetence at restraining themselves is so uncomfortable, that they toss their bracelet in a drawer (or perhaps angrily out of a window) and hope no one asks them about it ever again.

If you're feeling uncomfortable right now, good! That discomfort means you're progressing. You're right on track; just stay with it. Remember the words of theologian Charles H. Spurgeon: "By perseverance the snail reached the ark." Re-

VOICES

I had reached a point in my career where I realized I had to improve my attitude on the job. One day at work, I phoned my wife and asked her to pick up some self-improvement books for me while she was at the library.

When I got home that evening, there were six books on the counter waiting for me. As I thumbed through each in turn, one book really caught my attention: A Complaint Free World, *by Will Bowen. I really liked the message it communicated. The stories were relatable, and I could not resist the challenge to go twenty-one days without complaining.*

I bought my own copy and began using a rubber band as my reminder. Several friends at work began to take the challenge. It became a game. We were texting each other asking what day we were on and sharing the encounters that had led us to reset our day count.

Soon, sharing a cup of coffee became a task. We had to train ourselves to choose our words carefully to avoid complaining or gossiping.

The best change occurred for me at home. One night my wife and I were kissing in the kitchen, and she asked me, "Have you noticed we have been kissing more than usual?"

We discovered that I used to come home and complain about work, which would put us both in a bad mood. This was not conducive to a loving relationship. My new approach of coming home and not complaining found us in a good mood and enjoying being together.

It took me almost six months to get my first twenty-one

> *days under my belt. I have changed the way I communicate*
> *with others, and this has made me a happier person. I listen to*
> *the book in my car frequently to keep myself on track.*
>
> —SHAWN O'CONNELL
>
> ALBUQUERQUE, NEW MEXICO

gardless of how snail-like your progress seems, you are moving toward your ideal and noticing your complaints, even if you can't yet stop them, which is an important step along the path.

I recently upgraded the operating system on the MacBook Pro laptop I am using to write this book. I've had this computer for several years and like it very much. However, the standard configuration of the new operating system reversed the orientation of the computer's track pad. Previously, to scroll down the screen I swiped my finger in a downward motion on the track pad. However, most touch screens now employ the opposite movement to simulate the sensation of actually moving the screen with your fingers, and this is how the updated OS set my track pad.

What irony to be writing about the Conscious Incompetence stage when this happened. After more than two years, I had to move my fingers in the opposite direction to scroll up or down. For several days my fingers

> "Whoever has the courage to shut up his sorrow within his own heart is stronger to fight against it than he who complains."
>
> **—GEORGE SAND**

habitually moved one way while the screen image slid counter to where I wanted. My frustration was palpable and distracting. I *knew* that the track pad orientation had changed. I *knew* that I was doing it wrong. I kept telling myself to remember to move my finger in the opposite direction, but it was no use. After two years of doing it a certain way, I was not going to change immediately. It took several uncomfortable days to retrain myself. I was hopelessly incompetent and very, very conscious of it.

It's been a week since I upgraded the operating system. My fingers now automatically slide in the new direction. I don't even have to think about it. In fact, it seems natural, as if it's the way I have always navigated documents. So, if it feels like you're at the stage where you notice your complaints and want so very badly to quell them but can't, just relax and know that in time, you will retrain yourself.

Be patient. Great benefits await you when you're making this change.

As we've discussed, complaining has caused you to focus on what is wrong, drawing your attention away from what you want while attracting what you don't want.

As such, complaining is damaging to relationships.

Complaining to someone lowers the energy in the relationship, and complaining about someone causes you to look for more to complain about in that person.

In 1938, Lewis Terman interviewed dozens of psychiatrists and counselors to identify a common thread in unhappy marriages. His research found that unhappy couples were distinguished from happy ones by the extent to which they reported their partner being argumentative, critical, and nagging (i.e., complaining).

"Complaining about the opposite sex will only bring you more crappy dates."

—ANNA MARIA TOSCO

In other words, *unhappy relationships are most often distinguished by how much complaining occurs within the relationship.*

Complaining warps, weakens, and sometimes even destroys the very relationships that could bring us happiness. When we engage in complaining, our relationships stagnate and devolve. Complaining shifts our focus from the positive attributes that drew us to the other person to what we perceive to be their faults. This shift draws us into a trap of feeling unfulfilled and can cause the other person to feel inadequate.

Further, complaining can cause us to seek out unhappy relationships and repeat negative patterns.

Anna Maria Tosco, who goes by the pen name "the Sassy Psychologist," wrote an article for *The Suburban* titled "Sex and the City Syndrome: How Complaining About the Opposite Sex Will Only Bring You More Crappy Dates," which explains how our negative views of relationships perpetuate negative connections.

Tosco states that complaining about dates and relationships, as the women did so frequently on the show *Sex and the City,* saying things such as "There are no good men out there," "All men cheat," and "Everyone I date will leave me eventually," causes the neurotransmitters in your brain to build bridges to those beliefs. Holding these beliefs then causes your body to produce chemicals that make you feel sad, depressed, and hopeless.

Tosco writes, "If this type of thought persists for long periods of time, the body gets accustomed to the chemicals produced and will actually crave them, just like an addict craves his/her drug of choice. Your thought-derived chemical becomes an addictive substance and any interruption in this chemical firing will result in discomfort similar to . . . you guessed it: withdrawal symptoms."

She goes on to write, "Complaining about your relationships in a constant and persistent pattern will create chemicals to which you will become addicted. What is most fascinating and hard to believe is that once addicted, you'll subconsciously crave those bad dates, insensitive men, societal pressure, and annoying relationship clichés just to get a hit."

I know of a group of women who gather each week for what they call "Group Therapy." They meet at a Mexican restaurant to drink margaritas and complain about men. From what I'm told, their underlying theme is "All men are dogs!"

Well, if you've just spent several hours complaining to your friends that the man in your life is a dog, it's not surprising that you see Old Yeller sitting in the La-Z-Boy when you get home. Your mind looks for validation for what you have been saying. Your complaints become an unpleasant self-fulfilling prophecy.

Not one of these Group Therapy women is in a happy

and fulfilling relationship with a man. Do they want a satisfying relationship? Of course, but through their complaints they are sending out energetic vibrations that "men are dogs," causing them to look for and attract men with doglike behavior.

They are creating their reality with their complaints because their body releases chemicals that cause them to seek out similar negative experiences.

Bestselling author and spiritual teacher Eckhart Tolle explains that everyone has what he calls a pain-body. The pain-body is that part of us that gets a rush from hearing bad news, complaining about relationships, or being in a confrontation with someone. Uncomfortable as these feelings may be, they are nonetheless stimulating, and some people get addicted to this negativity. It's like a drug they can't live without.

There is a term for this: pain addiction. When you experience pain, either real or imagined, your body squirts a shot of endorphins into your bloodstream. Endorphins are endogenous morphine, a powerful narcotic that is produced by your body's own natural apothecary. This anesthetic is released when you experience pain, and complaining ignites emotional pain.

It goes like this: Complaining triggers pain, pain triggers endorphins, and endorphins get you high. You probably don't notice this elevated state any more than a heavy coffee drinker notices a caffeine rush, but just as the coffee drinker trying to kick caffeine will experience withdrawal, so, too, will the person who is giving up complaining.

With regard to relationships, remember that both you and the other person have a proclivity to activate your pain-body to produce a shot of endorphins. This understanding alone can help you regain your sanity during an uncomfortable exchange.

The common factor in unhappy relationships is that one or both people complain regularly to or about the other person. Complaining is draining and unfulfilling, and it makes you feel agitated and even defensive.

Several years ago, I was doing an interview with an Australian magazine when the journalist asked, "So, Will, how does one create a happy relationship?" To which I replied, "Take two happy people and put them together—it's the only way it works."

This is why the greatest gift you can give someone with whom you are in a relationship is the gift of your happiness, to strive to become a glass-is-half-full person and be grateful for what you have rather than complaining, which is literally contagious for the other person.

But I have to warn you that as you become Complaint Free, you can't expect everyone else around you to silence their complaints immediately. Again, to liken complaining to a drug, many of us have been in situations where other people were drinking excessively, smoking, or doing drugs. If someone chooses not to go along with the group, the individuals in the group feel threatened. My personal theory regarding this phenomenon is that people engaging in destructive behaviors know that

"Complaints are like the clouds that produce no rain no matter how thick they gather."

—ISRAELMORE AYIVOR

they are not acting in their best interest, and this knowledge is magnified in the presence of someone who is showing restraint and not partaking.

Only share your Complaint Free journey with people you know will support you and avoid telling those who might deter you—because they will most certainly try!

In 1967, a study was done with rhesus monkeys that reflects this tendency in human beings. A single toy was placed in a cage of monkeys and whenever one of them approached the toy, that monkey was punished (exactly how it was punished is not disclosed).

When a new monkey, one that had *not* been punished for trying to get the toy, was placed in the cage, the monkeys who had been punished attacked it whenever it went for the toy. Most notably, when another new monkey was then added to the cage, even the monkey that had never been punished would attack the newcomer if it approached the toy.

Friends, family, co-workers, even acquaintances are threatened when we try to break out of the pack—when we go for a toy such as a better life by giving up complaining. Although you are attempting to do something in your best interest, many will attempt to thwart your efforts. In those moments, it's a good idea to see those people as sacred clowns.

What's a sacred clown?

Throughout their histories, most Native American tribes have had sacred clowns. Most of us are familiar with the tribal chief and the medicine man, but few have heard of sacred clowns. The sacred clown is an agent of intentional chaos. Their role is to create problems for members of the tribe as a way of getting them to maintain focus during hardship and to develop mental toughness.

The Lakota people call sacred clowns Heyokas. Among the Pueblo tribes of the Southwest, the Zuni refer to them as Mudheads, and the Hopi call them Hanos. The Apache call them Libayes. The Cheyenne refer to them as Contraries. Some tribes call them Thunder Dreamers because to become a sacred clown, a brave must first have a dream about thunder. Once this happens, the young brave is separated from his family and taken to live with a mentor who trains him in the ancient ways of being an antagonist to the others. Before becoming a great chief, the venerable Crazy Horse was himself a Thunder Dreamer.

It's a sacred clown's esteemed role to bother, agitate, irritate, distract, and generally wreak havoc upon the other members of the tribe. For example, if a brave kills a deer and brings it back to the camp, the sacred clown might sneak up and steal the game and then drag it off into the woods, where it will be eaten by wolves or coyotes. If a woman builds a fire, the sacred clown may wait until she goes to get water and then kick the fire over and stomp it out.

Native American scholar Gil Nichols explained to me the

role of sacred clowns, saying, "As an agent of divine chaos, most Native Americans believe that sacred clowns were the first thing created by the Great Spirit.

"A single twig breaks, but the bundle of twigs is strong."

—TECUMSEH

Anything the clown could do to irritate others and thereby shock them out of their complacency is employed. They will mess with the other members of the tribe given any chance that arises. And it's not considered a bad thing but rather an honor when the sacred clown chooses you as the target of his attacks."

Even today, sacred clowns make an annual appearance at the hallowed Sun Dance on the Pine Ridge Reservation in the Black Hills of South Dakota. The Sun Dance is a timeless tradition held every August during which, for four grueling days, braves perform the steps of their ancestors under a sweltering summer sun without food or water.

Some of the dancers even elevate this ritual to self-mutilation, just as their ancestors did, by cutting their chests in two vertical stripes atop each pectoral muscle and then sliding an elk bone in one incision and out the other. They then lash themselves to a ceremonial tree with ropes tied to the bone tips protruding from their lacerated skin. Back and forth these men sway in the blistering heat, staring up into the sun while slipping into a state of divine madness. You may remember a similar ritual depicted in the 1970 movie *A Man Called Horse*.

The pain is excruciating, and dancing without food or water is exhausting. Forget triathlons; this is the ultimate test of endurance for any human!

On the third day, when the dancers are depleted, dehydrated, questioning their resolve, and seriously considering giving up, the clowns, dressed in traditional black and white, make their appearance.

While the dancers struggle to maintain both their commitment and their sanity, the clowns jump around shrieking and taunting them. In years past, sacred clowns would mount a horse facing backward and ride through the dancers, nearly trampling them. During modern Sun Dances the horses have been replaced with ATVs. Because the dancers have taken an oath not to eat or drink during the Sun Dance, the clowns may wave a hamburger under their nose, encouraging them to break their fast, or they may shoot them with giant squirt guns. They will insult the dancers, telling them they're too weak to continue and should just give up.

Now, you might think that the sacred clowns' harassment of the dancers would demoralize and weaken the dancing braves' resolve, but it causes them to redouble their commitment and dig deep for strength and resilience.

But why do the sacred clowns wait to show up until the third day of the dance?

Gil Nichols explains, "For the first couple of days, the dancers are excited for the ritual and their adrenaline keeps them going. But by the third day they are physically, emotionally, spiritually, and mentally exhausted. By tormenting them when they are at their lowest, the clowns set off an explosion of energy and clarity that keeps them going."

Does it work?

In 2013, I went to the Pine Ridge Reservation to spend time with two modern-day sacred clowns, and they told me a story of what had happened just two years prior.

That year there was an agreement that sacred clowns from another tribe would show up to harass the dancers on the third day of the Sun Dance, but for some reason, there was some confusion about the scheduling and none showed up. As a result, for the first time in the history of the dance, three braves had to be hospitalized due to heat exhaustion. With no one to force them to tap into the deep reservoirs of strength, commitment, and energy within, the dancers succumbed to the brutal heat, lack of water, and exhausting dancing, and several nearly died.

So rather than resenting the people who chide you for taking the Complaint Free challenge, reframe them in your mind as sacred clowns and give thanks for them. Let their teasing, skepticism, and harangues be motivators to intensify your resolution to keep going rather than convincing you to give up.

If you want to be a frigate bird rather than a seagull, remember that the frigate bird only goes higher when it faces into the wind. It's the *resistance* of the air currents that lifts the frigate bird upward and keeps it moving forward, and you can choose to let resistance do the same for you. Expect resistance from others but know that as you become a happier person, the very same people who resisted you will soon regard you with admiration.

You can allow their resistance to defeat you, or you can let it complete you. The choice is yours.

As you are making your Complaint Free transformation, it is vitally important for you to choose carefully who you will spend your time with, because, believe it or not, you are the aggregate total of the five people you spend the most time with. Take a moment to let that sink in. If you're around a bunch of negative, complaining people, you will, by default, mirror both their emotions and their words.

This is because of your brain's mirror neurons.

Mirror neurons cause the same synapses to fire in your brain when you watch or hear someone else experience something. They literally mirror the same state, and this explains why you wince in pain when you see someone else accidentally cut their finger—your brain fires off as if it were your finger that had just been sliced.

Repeated exposure to a negative person causes the mirror neurons in your mind to feel the same state the complaining person is feeling, and soon you become as negative and complaining as them.

We humans are like clock pendulums.

In 1665, Dutch physicist Christiaan Huygens, the inventor of the pendulum clock, was lying in bed with a minor illness and watching two of his clocks hanging on a wall. He decided

to try a little experiment, so
he got up and started each
clock's pendulum swing-
ing at a different time. He
then lay back down and

"I am the one thing in life
I can control."

—LIN-MANUEL MIRANDA,
HAMILTON

watched. To his surprise, within a half hour both pendulums
synchronized and began to swing back and forth at the exact
same rate, as if they had been started together. No matter how
many times or with how many clocks Huygens tried this, the
pendulums all synced up within thirty minutes.

It is the nature of both clocks and people to sync up over
time.

This is called entrainment. With regard to people, *entrain*
means "draw along with oneself"; to be entrained is to be
swept along in the flow of another person.

Have you noticed that when you're part of an audience and
everyone begins to applaud, if the applause lasts long enough,
the clapping will establish a rhythm until everyone applauds
to the same beat? The clapping may have begun scattered and
random, but if it continues for a significant period, it, just like
the clock pendulums, will sync up.

Entrainment is a principle just as gravity is a principle
and is, therefore, neither good nor bad—it simply is. And just
like gravity, it's always working. You are constantly syncing
up with those around you. You are being entrained by them,
and they are being entrained by you. When you are around
others who complain, you will find yourself tending to com-

plain more often. But the good news is that when you begin to complain less frequently, those around you will be entrained by you and start to complain less in your presence.

So take a look at who you are spending your time with and make a commitment to spend time with people who are happy and not chronic complainers. Seek out the happiest person you can find and invite them out for coffee or lunch. Who knows? They may introduce you to some of their upbeat friends and soon you'll develop a whole network of happy, noncomplaining people.

This is important because, as I said earlier, you are the total of the five people you spend the most time with.

Be warned: If it seems like everyone you know is negative and complaining, then I've got some sobering news for you—you probably are as well. As Richard Bach wrote in *Illusions,* "Like attracts like." You're in this nest of complainers because you, too, are a complainer. But don't feel bad. If most of the people you know are negative, that actually makes you normal.

When I was striving to go twenty-one consecutive days without complaining, I found that after a month or so I could string together several days in a row without complaining. Then I would get a call from my friend Tom (not his real name) and he would draw me into a slew of complaints.

After one conversation during which I switched my bracelet four times, I told a mutual friend, "I'm going to have to avoid Tom until I make the twenty-one days Complaint Free. His negativity is so contagious that I fall into complaining every time we speak."

"Hmmm," she said. "I've never noticed Tom to be negative."

"You haven't?" I asked.

"No," she said. "He's usually cheerful and offers optimistic observations about what's going on in his life and mine, too."

That took a moment to sink in. Perhaps *my* default mode of communication with Tom was complaining. The next time he called, I resolved to sit in absolute silence if necessary, rather than complain. I didn't complain, and surprisingly, neither did he.

The comic strip character Pogo was right when he said, "We have met the enemy and he is us." When I stopped complaining to Tom, our conversations ceased to be a fertile ground for negativity.

If you're unhappy in your relationships, you need to take an honest look and see just how much complaining is going on and what's really behind the complaints.

In "A Descriptive Taxonomy of Couples' Complaint Interactions," Dr. J. K. Alberts reports, "Diverse research indicates that negativity and negative communication are positively correlated with relational dissatisfaction." That's a fancy way of saying that unhappy couples, be they friends or lovers, complain a lot!

You may think that the complaints that show up in your relationships are unique. However, according to Dr. Alberts there are five broad categories of dissatisfaction that lead to people griping about one another:

DISSATISFACTION	EXAMPLE
1. Behavior (the person's actions or lack thereof)	"You left your socks on the floor again, as usual! Why do you always do that?"
2. Personal characteristics (their personality or beliefs)	"You're a loudmouth; you talk nonstop and never listen to other people!"
3. Performance (the way their actions are performed)	"You're not planting that tree right; don't you know that you should dig the hole deeper?"
4. Complaining (the other person's own griping)	"You are always whining at me about something!"
5. Personal appearance	"Your hair is a mess; did you even bother to run a comb through it this morning?"

Of the five dissatisfaction categories, Alberts discovered that complaints about behavior accounted for fully 72 percent of all griping done in relationships.

Think about that. Nearly three-fourths of all the complaints spoken in relationships are about what the other person does or does not do. In fact, Alberts found that people complain about behavior nearly five times more often than the next-highest reason (personal characteristics, 17 percent) and three times more than all the other characteristics combined!

Why do we do this? Because we mistakenly believe that our complaints will induce the person to change their behavior. But you have never complained anyone, including yourself, into positive change. Rather, when you complain to someone, you define that person as one who engages in the behavior you are complaining about and they are more, not less, likely to repeat it.

When you say, "You always leave your socks on the floor," it's like a *Star Wars* Jedi mind trick. Your comment registers in the other person's psyche, defining them as someone who deposits dirty socks on the floor, and that perpetuates the behavior. It is far better to ask the other person for what you want and then praise them when they begin to act even remotely as you would like.

So, what's the best way to get others to do what you want without complaining?

Dr. Marsha M. Linehan, the developer of dialectical behavior therapy, recommends what she calls the DEARMAN approach. Here's how she describes the process in the *DBT Skills Training Handouts and Worksheets* workbook:

DEARMAN	
Describe the situation. Stick to the facts using a neutral rather than accusatory or critical tone of voice.	"You left your socks on the floor."
Express your feelings. Say how this affects you.	"When you do that, I feel upset because I think you expect me to pick up your dirty clothes."
Assert what you want using words such as *I want* or *I would like* rather than *I don't want* or *You shouldn't*.	"After you take your socks off, I'd like you to put them in the hamper."
Reinforce (reward) the person ahead of time.	"I'd be happier and much easier to live with if you would do that."

Mindful: In your own mind, reinforce your goal of having a happy, healthy, Complaint Free relationship. Don't get caught up in attacks or distractions.

Appear confident by maintaining eye contact and using a calm, even tone of voice.

Negotiate if necessary. If the person responds, "I will pick up my socks later," get an agreement as to when "later" will be. For example: Is later in the next hour? Before bed? First thing in the morning? Get a specific commitment as to when your request will be met.

And most important of all, don't complain to someone else. Not only will this not result in the change you seek, but if the other person ever finds out that you were

"It is impossible to suffer without making someone pay for it; every complaint already contains revenge."

—FRIEDRICH NIETZSCHE

complaining about them, they are more likely to stick with the negative behavior just for spite because they feel embarrassed.

A married couple I'll call Rowland and Lorraine met another couple who had a young son about the same age as their daughter. The adults had a lot in common and the kids loved playing together, so the families began to spend a lot of time hanging out. Over the course of several months, both Rowland and Lorraine found that they started to dread these little gatherings until finally Lorraine said, "I really like those two when they're a couple, but whenever she and I are alone all she does is complain about him."

Rowland laughed. "He does the same thing when it's just him and me. He gripes constantly about her, too. Not only that, he also seems intent on digging up any problems you and I might be having. I feel like he's trying to stir up trouble between you and me."

Over time, Rowland and Lorraine began to avoid the other couple, which was sad for everyone, including the kids. But the real tragedy was that the other couple never spoke to each other about their problems, which means that the problems didn't get solved.

Becoming Complaint Free means beginning to practice

healthy communication skills. It's important to remember that speaking directly to someone to resolve an issue with them is not complaining. If you purchase something from an online retailer and there is a problem with your order, it's not complaining to reach out to them and ask that they make it right. If you're having an issue with another person, it's not complaining to speak to them about it (ideally using the DEAR-MAN method) so long as you stick to the facts, and as we've discussed previously, facts are always neutral. Speaking to the company or person who can resolve your issue is not complaining, it is a *request for accountability*.

Complaining to someone other than the person with whom you have a problem is called triangulation, and it perpetuates problems in relationships rather than solving them.

In my opinion, relationships serve two primary purposes:

1. Fun
2. Growth

Fun is the pleasure we derive from being with the other person. Growth comes from the relationship's calling up un-healed issues within ourselves. When we are with someone for a prolonged period, our old stuff *will* come up. And this is normal. There's a line in the song "Don't Worry 'Bout a Thing" by the band SHeDAISY, "We all got a little junk in the trunk," and relationships help us grow by opening up our trunks so we can deal with the junk.

Unfortunately, rather than dealing with issues by taking

them up with the person with whom they're in a relationship, most people blame the other person and complain to friends to validate being a victim. As bestselling author Gay Hendricks puts it, "Most couples fight in an attempt to assume an unfair share of the victimhood." In doing so, they miss a great opportunity to deepen the relationship and clean the junk out of their own trunk.

To enjoy Complaint Free relationships, remember that all relationships will bring up issues within you that you then get to work on. Embrace this opportunity and become a happier, more emotionally healthy person.

And above all, don't wait for other people to stop complaining for you to successfully complete the twenty-one-day challenge. Become a Complaint Free person yourself and you will inspire others around you to stop complaining while simultaneously attracting people who are more upbeat and optimistic.

The change you seek is never "out there," it is within. Saint Francis of Assisi put it this way: "What you are looking for is what is looking."

CHAPTER 4

WHY WE COMPLAIN

Negativity can only feed on negativity.
−DR. ELISABETH KÜBLER-ROSS

Author Russell Brunson writes that everything we human beings do is driven by a desire for increased status. Now, when you hear the word *status* you probably think of it as the esteem other people have for us, and that plays into it, but Brunson is talking about the way we define ourselves.

We all have a concept of who we would like to be in the world, and every decision we make—about our hairstyle, the person we date, the car we drive, the friends we associate with, the causes we support, where we live, whether or not we have a dog (and if we do, the size, color, and breed of the dog), the clothes we wear, even whether or not we get a piercing or a tattoo—plays into our internal sense of status.

Status is defined as our relative position compared to other people. Status is how we stack up against others based on what we value for ourselves. For example, the man who grows his hair long, wears tie-dye, and drives a vintage Volkswagen

VOICES

I first learned of this wonderful program on the Today *show. I began asking my coworkers if they would be interested in doing this. The majority of them agreed and we ordered our bracelets. We decided that while we were waiting for them to arrive, we would set one day of our business week aside and try not to complain on that given day. We now set Mondays aside as NO MOAN MONDAYS.*

We have signs posted on our company bulletin board and around the office to remind employees to try not to moan, gripe, or complain on Mondays. It really has been an inspiration in our office and we usually greet each other on Mondays with "Welcome to No Moan Monday!"

When you think about it, life is just too short. We are always looking for those big blessings in life (e.g., more money, job security, weight loss, etc.), but we need to start looking for those tiny blessings that are given to us each day.

I think this program is wonderful. We are so blessed!

—SALLY SCUDIERE

KENT, OHIO

microbus has decided that his choices make his status superior to that of a man who chooses to wear Gucci and drives a Rolls-Royce. It's all a series of decisions, and because status is based on personal beliefs, each of the men in this example sees himself as having increased status over the other.

Social status is a major contributing factor because the esteem that other people have for us reinforces our feeling of personal status. Human beings are social animals and we have a need to be part of what we consider to be our herd. Our relative position within that herd is reflected back to us by how others treat us.

Complaining plays a vital role in helping to either maintain or elevate our social status. Dr. Kowalski, the psychology professor I mentioned previously, identified five reasons that people complain, and all of them impact our status among others. As you hear yourself and other people complain, you'll find that all complaints are spoken for one or a combination of these five reasons.

To make the five reasons people complain easier to understand and remember, I've taken Kowalski's research and created the following mnemonic device. Just remember that people complain to GRIPE:

Get attention
Remove responsibility
Inspire envy
Power
Excuse poor performance

Get Attention

Human beings have an innate need to be acknowledged by other people. This need for attention is not a negative thing. Attention from others makes us feel safe, secure, and cared for. Being recognized by others makes us feel like we belong, that we are part of the tribe. People will often complain simply because they want attention from others and can't think of another, more positive means of getting the notice they crave.

On an episode of *Magic for Humans*, Justin Willman demonstrated perfectly this inherent need people have for getting attention. Willman hired dozens of actors, assigned each of them a role, and placed them in a remote corner of a public park. Some examples: A man and woman were assigned to play the role of two young lovers having a picnic, several teens were assigned the role of Frisbee players, two men were assigned to play chess together, a woman played the part of a person sitting alone on a blanket reading a book. Just as if they were in a movie, each of the actors was given a part to play to make that corner of the park look like it was filled with regular people enjoying a warm spring afternoon.

Willman waited until a man who was not one of the actors walked nearby, and at that precise moment he stood up and shouted, "Everyone! Gather around, my name is Justin Willman and I'm a magician." Both the actors and the man who was not in on the scheme began to walk slowly toward Willman.

Willman continued, "I'm going to show you all an amazing trick and to do so I'm going to need a volunteer from the audience." He then scanned the assembled group before selecting the man who had been strolling by and said, "You, sir, please help me with my illusion." The man shrugged and walked up

to Willman as the actors ap-
plauded his participation.
Willman placed a chair on
the ground as his actors
began to crowd closer to the

"There is no way to use the word
'reality' without quotation marks
around it."

—JOSEPH CAMPBELL

scene. Willman then instructed the man to sit in the chair.

"I'm going to make this man disappear right before your very eyes," Willman cried. As the actors expressed varying degrees of doubt, Willman covered the man with a tarp. After saying a few "magic" words, Willman yanked the tarp off the man, and the actors, just as they had been trained, gasped in amazement!

"Where did he go?" asked one.

"How did you do that?" said another.

"That's amazing!" said a third, as every one of the actors made similar comments of surprise and stunned bewilderment over the man's having just "disappeared."

Of course, the man hadn't disappeared, he was sitting right there in the chair, but the actors were so convincing that he believed he was now invisible. An enormous grin spread over his face as he looked at his hands and feet. He could see himself but he reasoned that no one else could, and he was thrilled! He was invisible! How exciting!

Soon, the actors dispersed to resume their roles as park attendees while the "invisible" man began to walk among them. He ambled up to people and waved his hands in front of their faces, trying to get a reaction, but the well-trained actors simply stared past him. The man snagged a Frisbee out of the air and the teen who had thrown it reacted with surprise and confusion. Mr. Invisible walked over to the actor couple having a picnic, opened their basket, and withdrew food from it, and the couple jumped up as if they had seen the actions of a ghost.

All the while, the man's huge smile never dimmed. He was having a blast!

The invisible man's enjoyment continued . . . but only for about six minutes. Slowly his elation over being invisible began to dim. The expression on his face changed from "Hooray! I'm invisible. Nobody can see me!" to a look of terror that read, "Oh my God! Nobody can see me!"

In that moment, his desire for obscurity and anonymity was replaced by the very real human need to get attention from others.

Getting attention from others is not a human want, it's a human *need*!

The weather, work, their intimate partner, their children, the economy, and local sports teams are favorite topics of people complaining just to get attention—to start a conversation. What this type of complainer is really saying is "Hey, notice me! I want to talk to you. I want to get your attention and I'm completely lost as to what to say other than to gripe about something."

If there is someone at work who tends to come into your workspace frequently to complain, consider that they might just want attention. Then take direct action by asking a question before they have a chance to complain. Ask about the person's hobbies, family, health, etc. Give attention to this person first, so they don't feel the need to come and solicit it through complaining.

> "The mind is its own place and in it self, can make a Heav'n of Hell, a Hell of Heav'n."
>
> **—JOHN MILTON**

You might think, "I don't have time for that." Well, do you have time for your co-worker's continually coming to you with complaints? Are you committed to changing your association with this person?

Here's a great technique to get the conversation off on a positive note. Ask, "What's going well with [you, your family, your work, your hobby, etc.]?"

Out of habit, the compulsive complainer will probably respond by telling you what is *not* going well with regard to whatever topic you threw out. This person is so accustomed to griping to get attention that it never occurs to them that it's possible to have a positive connection with someone. Rather than fighting this response, accept it. Consider this to be like training a parrot to speak. It will take patience and repeated effort, but it's worth it to establish a new mode of communication with the person.

When your co-worker starts to complain, smile and delicately interrupt, asking again, "Yes, but what is going *well* with . . ." Or "Yes, but what do you *like* about . . ." Or "Yes, but how would you *ideally* like to see this working out?"

Just as it can take many weeks of switching your bracelet to complete one full Complaint Free day, it may take several redirections on your part to get your co-worker to even consider that there are, indeed, some good aspects to their life. Be patient and have compassion. Remember that this type of complainer lives in fear that not griping will mean not being able to get attention from other people.

When I was a young boy, I used to hang out in my grandfather's hardware store in Manning, South Carolina. There were a half dozen men who worked there as clerks, but my favorite was a guy named Willie. Willie always seemed to have a way of charming the customers and making whatever interaction he had with them pleasant and positive.

Rather than saying the typical things most clerks say, such as "What brings you in today?" or "How can I help you?" Willie always mustered up genuine enthusiasm and a broad smile and asked, "What's the good word, my friend?"

"What's the good word?" was calculated to get a positive response from the customer and it worked every time. I once watched a man storm into the store after another clerk had sold him several gallons of the wrong color of paint. You could feel the man's rage, but Willie melted it away with his verbal jujitsu by asking, "What's the good word?" The customer was completely taken aback. He stood for a moment pondering and then said, "Well . . . my daughter got married last weekend." Willie replied, "That's great, my friend, now let's get you the right color paint."

You can control other people's minds and attitudes by ask-

ing the right questions. Questions such as "What's going well?,"
"What's the good word?," "What are you happy about?," and
"What's the best thing that's happened to you so far today?"
change the complainer's mental track from negative to positive while still allowing them to get the attention they need.

Remove Responsibility

Something that negatively impacts our social status—and, as
a result, our personal status—is not measuring up to someone
else's expectations when completing a task or project. So, we
pre-excuse our lack of action by complaining about the circumstances surrounding the task to lower their expectations.
This is preemptive complaining that is designed to make it
seem like we can't be held accountable for our failing in our
attempt and, above all, it's not our fault.

This type of complainer says things like:

"What do you want from me?"

"It's impossible because . . ."

"I would, but . . ."

"You can't fight city hall."

"It's Marketing's fault."

"No one will help me."

"I would lose weight but
my husband and kids love
all these fattening foods."

This type of complainer
seeks to build a case for
their inaction or inability to

> "Responsibility: A detachable
> burden easily shifted to the
> shoulders of God, Fate, Fortune,
> Luck or one's neighbor. In the days
> of astrology it was customary to
> unload it upon a star."
>
> **—AMBROSE BIERCE**

achieve even before they try by painting a hopeless picture of the outcome. "There's no use so I'm not going to try," the complainer is saying. This type of complainer is soliciting agreement from those who hear their complaints to validate that victimhood.

They seek to blame other people and circumstances to justify their own lack of effort. They blame their parents, the economy, their lack of education, their age, other people, and anything that may seem plausible. They are consumed with blame.

In his book *The Presence Process*, Michael Brown accurately breaks down the word *blame* as to "be lame." A person who complains to blame the world and other people for their life is being lame; that person decides they are powerless to do things well and wants you to buy into their belief. Further, they will reject any suggestion you offer as to how things might be improved. These people don't want your suggestions, they want your agreement that they are an impotent, helpless victim.

It goes like this: The person complains to you about a problem, so you proffer a possible solution. The suggestion is immediately shot down by them with another complaint as to how it won't work. Again, you put forth something they might try, and this, too, is discounted. In his book *Games People Play*, Eric Berne refers to this as the "Why Don't You . . . Yes But" game. You suggest a solution—"Why don't you . . ."—and the person's immediate response is "Yes, but . . . ," and they then proceed to tell you all the reasons why your suggestion will not work.

People seeking to "be lame" can play this game for hours. Their goal is actually to wear you down. They are not looking for you to help figure out ways to accomplish a task or solve a problem. Based on their comments you might think so, but they're not. They are trying to get you to admit that the problem is irresolvable. They have constructed a case for why it cannot be done, and if you agree to their reasons, it justifies their inaction. They want to be removed from the responsibility of creating a solution and want you to validate their position.

The only way to help these people is not to join them in the "Why don't you . . . Yes, but" game.

Super-motivator Tony Robbins has a brilliant way of handling such people. I learned it at one of his seminars more than thirty years ago and have used it thousands of times since then; it surprises me each time how well it works. When a person says any variation of "It can't be done," your response should always be "If it *were* possible, how might you do it?" The key word in this sentence is *you,* which clearly implies *not me*. This is not my problem to try to solve because any solution I offer will be shot down as a way of confirming your unwillingness to take effective action. So, how might *you* do it?

When you read this, it may sound dismissive or so obviously manipulative that you wonder if the complaining person will accuse you of playing a mental trick on them. However, as I said, it works! As someone begins to pile on all the reasons why something can't be done, keep asking, "If it were possible, how might you do it?" This can open the complainer's mind to considering possibilities where once that person saw only limitations. They will begin to think of ways of accomplishing the task and shift focus to making it happen.

A man I know tried to curb his alcohol consumption, but whenever he hung out with his friends for game night there would be a lot of drinking and he would succumb. He would complain, "I'd cut down on my drinking but every time I go over to my friend's house the beer is flowing and I just give in."

I responded, "If it were possible to cut down on your drinking, how might you do it?" He stared back at me for a moment and then said, "Well, I guess I could take soda or water to my friend's house, or I could watch the game with different people." These were very good solutions and they were always available, but he complained as a smokescreen to remove himself from taking responsibility for his alcohol consumption.

In many African cultures they do not say "I'm sorry" if someone is facing a formidable task or if a person has experienced a problem. Rather, they say, *"Pole"* (pronounced "PO-lee"). There is no single English equivalent for this Swahili word, but the essence of *pole* is "I get that what you're going through is difficult and I know you have the ability to move through it successfully."

If asking, "If this were possible, how might you do it?" doesn't shift the complainer away from endlessly saying "Yes, but . . . ," simply say, "I get what you're going through is difficult and I know that you have the ability to move through

it successfully." This statement simultaneously con-
veys compassion while
leaving the solution where
it belongs: at the door of the
person complaining to be
removed of responsibility.

"If you say something is not possible, what you are really saying is, 'I don't want it.'"

—SADHGURU JAGGI VASUDEV

This works particularly well with children. Being told that they are capable of finding a solution, kids will often surprise you with their ingenuity in finding a way to solve their problems so that you don't have to constantly rescue them. It's been said that good parenting is teaching a child how to parent themselves, and kids only learn to do this by figuring out solutions on their own.

Inspire Envy

Remember that status is defined as our relative position compared to other people. In other words, without other people to compare ourselves to, we would not have status. So people complain to inspire envy from others, which is just another way of saying "brag"!

A person will complain about someone else as a way of implying that they themselves do not have the character flaw being complained about.

"My boss is so stupid" is a backhanded way of saying, "I'm smarter than my boss and if I were in charge things would be much better around here." "My husband is a slob" is the complainer bragging that she is neat. "She drives like a maniac" translates to "I am a great driver."

This is often unconscious on the part of the complainer. Your task is to help that person shift away from this need to magnify their status with negative comparisons. People complaining to inspire envy are actually trying to get you to admire them. They feel empty and so they attack someone else as a means of trying to make themselves look better by comparison.

This often backfires because in one study on complaining, researchers found that when someone complains about an attribute of another person, those hearing the complaint actually ascribe those attributes to the person doing the complaining. "She's lazy and not motivated" is heard by others as the complainer being lazy and not motivated.

People can also brag about their good fortune as a way of inflating their status. But in nearly all cultures it's considered rude to brag. So people *complain* about their good fortune in an attempt to elevate their status.

I have a friend whom I met for coffee once a week for more than a decade. He makes a lot of money and once bought a half-million-dollar boat. As we sat in the coffee shop, my friend noticed several of our friends at the next table, so he leaned back and said loudly, "You know, Will, when you spend a half million dollars on a boat you'd think it would come with a better trailer, right?" Of course, our other friends rushed over to ask him, "You bought a half-million-dollar boat?"

A few weeks later we were having coffee when my buddy noticed some other friends walking by and he reached into his pocket, extracted a boat key, and said, "You know, Will, it seems like when you spend a half million dollars on a boat that the key would come with a floating key ring." I sat dumbly trying to figure out exactly why someone would even bring a boat key to a coffee shop until I realized this was premeditated; he was prepared to brag via his complaints should we spot anyone he wanted to impress. He had raised his social status by complaining rather than bragging.

"Who knows himself a braggart, let him fear this, for it will come to pass that every braggart shall be found an ass."

—WILLIAM SHAKESPEARE

A popular phrase today is *flex culture*. Flex culture is just another name for conspicuous consumption, the act of trying to outshine others by purchasing goods or services to display wealth and inflate social status.

Gossip is complaining to inspire envy. When you gossip, you should switch your bracelet. The underlying message behind gossip is that the gossiper wants to improve their social status by implying they are superior to the person about whom they are spreading stories.

Gossip is speaking negatively about someone who is not present. To be clear, I'm not saying you can't talk about other people, but what I'm suggesting is that you:

1. Speak only about the positive traits of those who are absent.
2. Say the same things, using the same inflection, that you'd say if the person were present.

"But that takes all the fun out of it," many have whined to me.

Exactly. Gossips are not speaking to share information; they are pointing out what they perceive to be another's negative traits so as to appear superior by comparison.

One of the more interesting things I've discovered about complaining to inspire envy is that people brag not only about being or having the best; ironically, they also brag about having the worst. I once listened to a woman in a small airport harangue a couple sitting next to her about the terrible plight of living in her city. She went on and on about crime, pollution, and corruption in her town as the unfortunate man and woman nodded and shifted uncomfortably in their seats. It hit me that this woman was actually bragging about being able to bear all the challenges she related.

It reminded me of the skit "The Four Yorkshiremen" by Monty Python.

In this sketch, four sophisticated, well-dressed gentlemen from Yorkshire, England, are seated together enjoying some expensive wine. Their conversation begins with statements of shared gratitude for their successes, shifts subtly negative, and then, over time, the complaining one-upmanship becomes excessive to the point of hilarity.

One gentleman comments that, although he's wealthy now, as a young man he would have been lucky to afford the price of a cup of tea. A second gentleman, wanting to outdo the first, stated that he would have been fortunate to have purchased *cold* tea.

The others join in and the complaining revs up. Soon, their comments spiral into ludicrousness as each tries to prove that his early

"No one gossips about other people's secret virtues."

—BERTRAND RUSSELL

life was the one of greatest hardship. One of the gentlemen tells of the shabby condition of the house he lived in as a boy. The second clicks his tongue, rolls his eyes, and replies, "*House!* You were lucky to have a house! We used to live in one room, all twenty-six of us, no furniture, half the floor was missing, and we were all huddled together in one corner for fear of falling."

Back and forth the lamentations continue, growing more dismal each time, as another says, "Eh, you were lucky to have a room! We used to have to live in the corridor."

"Oh, we used to *dream* of living in a corridor!" says another. "We used to live in an old water tank on a rubbish tip. We got woken up every morning by having a load of rotting fish dumped all over us!"

"Well, when I say 'house' it was only a hole in the ground covered by a sheet of tarpaulin, but it was a house to us."

"We were evicted from our 'ole in the ground; we had to go and live in a lake."

"You were lucky to have a lake! There were a hundred and fifty of us living in a shoebox in the middle of the road!"

Finally, one of the gentlemen decides the competition has gone far enough, and he's going to win. With a determined look in his eyes he says, "All right then." Taking a deep breath and sitting up straight, he loudly states, "I had to get up in the morning, at ten o'clock at night, a half an hour before I went to bed, drink a cup of sulfuric acid, work twenty-nine hours a day down in a mill, and pay the mill owner for permission to come to work. And when we got home, our dad would kill us and dance about on our graves singing, 'Hallelujah!'"

As this sketch shows, complaining, even negative complaining, is a competitive sport! Complaints always go in one direction: toward greater severity, never the other way around. We would consider it insensitive if someone complained about something severe and another person responded by complaining about something minor. Complaining always escalates, and this is why it quickly gets out of hand.

The human propensity toward escalation was demonstrated in an interesting study. Two people were asked to face each other and one of them was instructed to gently grasp the forearm of the other. That person was then told to squeeze the other person's forearm. Next, the roles were switched and the second person was asked to squeeze the first person's forearm matching the exact same pressure they had received. Again, the roles were reversed with the same instructions: "Squeeze using the same pressure that the other person used when squeezing your arm." Back and forth they went as the researchers measured the amount of pressure applied. The scientists found that with each new squeeze, the participants applied pressure that was, on average, 14 percent *greater* than what they had received. This means that after only seven times of each person squeezing the other's arm, the pressure became twice as much as when the experiment began. This proves that it's simply an innate characteristic of people to increase severity, whether it's squeezing someone else's arm, arguing, or complaining.

"The power men possess to annoy me, I give them by a weak curiosity."

—RALPH WALDO EMERSON

People complaining or gossiping to inspire envy increase their comments in an attempt to get you to join in and agree with them. However, if you do, you're only inviting more, escalated complaints. Instead, take the focus off what the person is complaining about and put it where the complainer wishes it to be: on them! Strive to have the presence of mind to *compliment* the complainer for being the opposite of what they're complaining about.

If you're at work about to have a meeting and an employee named Phillip says, "We could start the meeting but Julie's late—as usual!" you should compliment Phillip for doing the opposite by saying, "You know what I appreciate about you, Phillip? You're always on time."

Don't explain why you are doing this; to do so would negate the power of this technique. Instead, listen for the core idea behind the complaint and compliment the complainer for being the polar opposite. Soon that person will feel that their status has been adequately elevated and they will have no need to complain about others to inspire envy.

Power

Nothing elevates social status like power, and complaints are the currency with which one purchases power.

What is power? Power is other people. The more people you have on your side, the more power you are perceived as having. A politician has power because they have the support and authority given to them by other people. Nothing is more important to a politician than moving voters out of the *undecided* category, because when people are neutral, they are not adding to one's political power, and nothing does this more effectively than complaining.

Imagine if I were to run for Senate here in Florida and my campaign commercial went like this:

> *Hi, I'm Will Bowen and I'm running for Senate here in the great state of Florida. I just want you to know that I think the politicians in Washington, D.C., are doing a great job. In fact, I wouldn't change a thing. So, elect me to the Senate so I can go up there and help keep things just the way they are. A vote for Bowen is a vote for the status quo!*

Would I get elected? Absolutely not! If a politician doesn't have complaints, they don't have a campaign. To build a base, politicians must get people upset! This is why over the last few decades political discourse has turned into political vitriol; it's the only way to stand out in an increasingly splintered media landscape.

I call this *enrage and engage*. Sadly, it's much easier to maintain someone's attention by making them angry than by presenting a vision of hope. This is unfortunate but true, and it goes back to the negativity bias we talked about earlier.

"Power is not a means; it is an end. One does not establish a dictatorship in order to safeguard a revolution; one makes the revolution in order to establish the dictatorship."

—GEORGE ORWELL

About ten years ago, I flew to Washington, D.C., to give a speech, and when I arrived, I went outside the airport to catch a shuttle to my hotel. The driver placed my bags in the back and held the van door open for me to enter. There was only one seat left, and as I slid into it, I noticed the man sitting next to me. His clothing concerned me.

It was a hot day in D.C., nearly ninety degrees, and yet my seatmate wore a heavy three-quarter-length wool coat, gloves that went all the way to his elbows, and not one but two ski masks. I was concerned because I'd just left the airport having been told that the terrorist threat level was at orange, and now here I was seated next to a terrorist poster boy.

And to make matters worse, he kept leaning over to me to ask, "Hey, buddy, what time is it?"

"It's time to get the heck out of this van," I thought to myself.

In time it came to light that he was an author and he was running late for a radio interview. I shared with him that I, too, was an author and asked about the book he was promoting.

He said he worked for one of the two major U.S. political parties and his job was to dig up everything negative about the other party's candidate. His research would be used by his candidate's campaign team to prepare negative ads to sway voters.

"I've written a how-to book on dirty campaigning," he said. He then asked, "So, what are your books about?" I stifled a laugh as I told him that my books were about the power of *not* complaining. A prolonged silence followed.

Wanting to change the subject, I asked, "It's really warm today, why are you dressed in such heavy clothes?"

"It's the strangest thing," he explained. "I used to live here in Washington, but I now have to live in Florida. When I'm here, I'm prone to convulsive, gasping asthma attacks. I have to dress this way or else I'll react to something in the air in D.C. and won't be able to breathe."

As we pulled up to his hotel, I thought to myself, "How interesting . . . your job is to foul the airwaves and you can't breathe. Buddy, you make your own lunch!"

Not only is politics driven by complaining, but so is all media—especially social media.

If you've not watched the movie *The Social Dilemma,* I highly recommend it. Former high-ranking officials from You-Tube, Facebook, Twitter, Instagram, and other social media platforms come clean about the algorithms they use to keep you hooked to their platforms for longer periods of time.

"Power does not corrupt. Fear corrupts . . . perhaps the fear of a loss of power."

—JOHN STEINBECK

What they've discovered is that if they can get you to watch something that aligns with your hobbies and interests, they can then suggest stories and videos that will slowly get you more and more enraged about something until you crave the content they are providing. The longer you expose yourself to their platform, the more advertisers can gain access to you and the more money the social media giants can make.

We have much to thank Steve Jobs for, not the least of which is the smartphone. But I wonder if Jobs appreciated the monster he was letting out of the cage when he introduced the first iPhone back in 2007, because smartphones are the number one purveyor of complaints and outrage.

Why? Because they're always with us and they are increasingly designed to hook us for longer periods of time. According to the online Cambridge Dictionary, the People's Word of 2018 was *nomophobia,* a term that describes the fear of being without your smartphone. According to Reviews.org, 75 percent of Americans say they're addicted to their phones and over 65 percent admit to sleeping with their phones. The average adult spends nearly 70 percent of their waking time (eleven hours every day) staring at screens. And people in research studies who were separated from their smartphones for as little as ten minutes showed signs of moderate to severe anxiety just like an addict being denied a drug. Scary, isn't it?

Our increasing addiction to our phones has dire consequences.

According to a *Journal of the American Medical Association* study, smartphone-addicted individuals experience increased loneliness, which can have serious mental and physical health implications, including poor sleep quality and reduced immune system function. Once smartphone users fall into a pattern of frequently monitoring negative news, their mood only worsens and their anxiety increases as they spiral down into what is commonly called "doomscrolling."

Our phones are our primary portal to "news" and social media, and studies have found that the more of these two we consume, the more unhappy and anxious we become.

When it comes to social media, this increased mental strain makes sense if you really think about it.

As mentioned previously, I currently live in Key Largo, Florida, which is a tropical island one hour south of Miami. One of the things people in Key Largo regularly do is gather by the bay to enjoy the glorious sunsets.

The other day I took my mini goldendoodle Ted E. Bear over to the park to watch a sunset. As the sun changed from blazing white, to muted yellow, and finally to a cascading mixture of fiery red and orange mixed with shades of blue before slipping beneath the sea, I took a picture of Ted in front of the sunset and posted it on Facebook. Well, that's not entirely true.

I actually took *dozens* of these pictures, then I went through them all to find one that was particularly excep-tional. Next, I cropped the photo and added a filter to

"There are only two industries that call their customers 'users': illegal drugs and software."

—EDWARD TUFTE,
THE SOCIAL DILEMMA

make it even more spectacular. *Then* I posted it. And that's what we all do with social media.

In our attempt to elevate our social status, we post the best augmented, and sometimes artificial, version of our lives. As a result, our friends, family, fans, and followers view our photos and think we are living lives that are much bet-ter than their own. This leads to a universal feeling of inad-equacy. "My life is nowhere near as good as that person's," we think, all the while forgetting that their images were selected for maximum perfection and then enhanced to make them look even better.

Excessive social media use causes us to fall into what I call Gobel syndrome. Comedian George Gobel was once booked on *The Tonight Show Starring Johnny Carson* on the same night as Bob Hope and Dean Martin—two of the biggest stars in the world at the time. Gobel looked at the megastars seated next to him and observed, "Did you ever get the feeling that the world was a tuxedo and you're a pair of brown shoes?"

In our attempt to make ourselves look better on social media, we make other people feel inadequate, like a pair of brown shoes in a tuxedo world. And the same holds true for us. When I look at all the exciting trips, restaurants, Broadway plays, and family events my literary agent Steve Hanselman posts on Facebook, I find myself feeling that my life is somehow inadequate compared to his, and I shift from being grateful for all the blessings I have to feeling envious and meager by comparison.

Social media facilitates comparison and complaining because it taps into our innate insecurities and fears. Traditional media is fueled by complaining for the same reasons. Remember the CRISIS! vs. GREAT NEWS! headlines I mentioned in the introduction? Upsetting news keeps us reading or tuning in so the media can sell more ads. The goal is to keep you engaged as often and for as long as possible, and complaining ensures this will happen.

Alisyn Camerota, former Fox News host who later moved over to CNN, said in an interview on the podcast *Fiasco* regarding her time at Fox News, "We did train the audience to become outraged. Often the scripts would say, 'You'll be outraged, right after the commercial.' We told people, stick around for the outrage, we told them they would be outraged, we told them afterward we're sure they're outraged, and, lo and behold, they became outraged." Which means their viewers were engaged for longer periods of time, giving advertisers more opportunities to pitch them products. Enrage and engage works every time.

In a 1968 movie titled *What's So Bad About Feeling Good?* a happiness virus begins to spread throughout New York City, infecting most of the city's residents. Rather than celebrating

this positive change in people, both city and national
officials grow fearful.

> "Habit is habit, and not to be flung
> out of the window by any man,
> but coaxed downstairs one step at
> a time."
>
> —MARK TWAIN

Government leaders de-
termine that the spread of
the virus threatens the eco-
nomic lifeblood of the city because residents suddenly stop
buying alcohol, tobacco, and drugs, resulting in the stock exchange and business districts being threatened with collapse
if everyone is happy and nice to one another.

Although this movie is fiction, it points to a great truth:
Contrary to what they say, those in authority do *not* want you
happy and Complaint Free because it threatens their power.

Here's what you can do to regain the power in your own
life:

1. If you have not done so already, *turn off ALL alerts and
   notifications* on your smartphone, computer, and tab-
   let. Do it *NOW*! By the way, did you notice that most
   software apps have shifted away from calling such in-
   terruptions "alerts" to now calling them "notifications"?
   This is because no one wants to be alerted, but everyone wants to be notified. Turn them off! And whenever
   you add a new app, select *No* when asked if you want
   notifications. You check your phone often enough already!

2. *Turn off* your phone, or put it on "Focus" mode whenever you're working or hanging out with family or

friends, and *especially* when you're driving. Begin to break the habit of obsessively checking your phone. Using phones while driving results in more than one hundred thousand deaths worldwide every year. Notice how often you feel the addict's ache to check your phone and "white knuckle" it until the compulsion abates. Try leaving your phone off for longer periods of time. As Mark Twain suggested, coax your habit down the stairs rather than throwing it out the window.

3. Recognize when someone, and especially the media, is trying to harness your power by complaining to you. Don't sell your power and your precious time for the price of a complaint. If a person complains to you about a situation, remain silent, or change the subject. And if someone is complaining to you about someone else to try to build an alliance against that person, simply state, "It sounds like the two of you have a lot to talk about." This subtly lets the complainer know that you're not going to get involved, and if they have an issue with someone else, they should speak directly and only to that person.

Excuse Poor Performance

According to the National Institute of Mental Health, 75 percent of people report public speaking as their number one fear, with many saying they find standing on a stage and addressing an audience more frightening than death itself.

However, I don't think this is true. I say this because I and many other professional speakers I know not only don't fear public speaking, *we love it*! Why? Because we're confident that we're good at it. In my opinion, what people fear is not the act of speaking, it's the potential embarrassment that might come from talking to an audience. It's bad enough to be speaking to one person and say something we think is stupid, or to forget our train of thought, but public speaking affords us an opportunity to be embarrassed on a massive scale!

> "He that is good for making excuses is seldom good for anything else."
>
> **—ATTRIBUTED TO BEN FRANKLIN**

By my estimation, I've done approximately seven hundred fifty speeches over the last three decades and only once did I ever completely blow it. Unfortunately, of all the speeches I've done, that one sticks out in my mind the most and I still feel a cold sweat when I think about it.

I had given several speeches in just a few days and I guess I was on autopilot. I was not being mindful as I addressed this particular audience. I got lost as to what I had and had not said. I scrambled to find my place, and as the audience stared at me in bewilderment, fear gripped my body. My heart pounded and my mind went completely blank. Forget trying to regain my place in this presentation; in that moment I couldn't remember *any* of my speech. After what seemed like an eternity (actually less than a minute), I remembered where I was and continued, but I was internally devastated by what had just happened. My social status with that audience had crashed and I knew it. I was embarrassed and I felt miserable.

Our greatest fear is being embarrassed, and we'll do anything we can to hide our mistakes as a means of avoiding potential embarrassment. When we don't do well at something, complaining about other people and situations is the best way to excuse our poor performance.

Of the five reasons people complain, you can think of "Excuse poor performance" as the past tense of "Remove responsibility."

When someone is trying to remove responsibility, they are given a task and are afraid they won't measure up, so they complain about the circumstances surrounding the task to lower other people's expectations.

When someone is trying to excuse poor performance, they have attempted to do something and then fallen short. But rather than owning their lack of success, they blame someone else.

In other words, removing responsibility occurs *before* an attempt is made, whereas excusing poor performance happens *after* an attempt is made.

We hear this all the time. The politician who blames the media after losing an election. The golfer who duffs a shot and complains, "Someone coughed during my backswing." The person who's late for a meeting and blames traffic. The kid who is tardy for school and blames their mom for not waking them up on time.

Our need to maintain our social status is so strong that

we will point the finger at anyone and anything other than ourselves to excuse our poor performance.

"Ninety-nine percent of the failures come from people who have the habit of making excuses."

—GEORGE WASHINGTON CARVER

The sad thing is that this often works. If we can get the people to whom we are offering our excuse to agree with us that the failure is not our fault, not only can we regain our social status, but in some cases we can elevate it. We have now painted ourselves not as someone who failed but as a victim of something beyond our control.

Examples of complaining to excuse poor performance abound.

In 2003, while playing for the Chicago Cubs, baseball legend Sammy Sosa was caught using a corked bat during a game against the Tampa Bay Devil Rays. Cork is lighter than wood or aluminum, so it speeds up the batter's swing and can improve his timing. When Sosa was caught using the illegal bat, he complained that it was not his fault because someone had handed him a practice bat rather than a game bat.

Former British prime minister Boris Johnson was accused of using illegal drugs, and his excuse is legendary. Johnson admitted to trying cocaine only once while a student at Eton College. But he excused himself from responsibility by saying that when he tried to snort the drug he accidentally sneezed instead, blowing away all the cocaine.

One of the most outlandish excuses came from Derek McGlone, a music teacher in Scotland who hated his job so much that he called in repeatedly with excuses that, he said, kept him from coming to work. Once, he even blamed ash from a volcano fully seven hundred miles away in Iceland, which he claimed made him sick. McGlone's most egregious excuse was claiming vehicular homicide. McGlone said that he had accidentally struck and killed a little girl while driving, so of course, he should be let off teaching for a while. Luckily, this was just an excuse—there was no accident, no little girl, and no one was hurt.

To me, the best complaint to excuse poor behavior came from mega movie star Woody Harrelson. On April 8, 2009, Harrelson had just wrapped shooting on the movie *Zombieland* when he was accosted by a photographer at Tampa airport. After trying to get the journalist to stop snapping pictures, Harrelson hauled off and punched the guy. The photographer filed a complaint with the Port Authority.

In his testimony as to what had transpired, Harrelson explained, "I thought he was a zombie." He went on to say that he was so deep into the zombie-slaying character he had been portraying for the movie that he thought the photographer was one of the undead flesh eaters, so he simply punched the guy out.

"It's not my fault" is the underlying message of a person complaining to excuse their poor performance. It is a desperate, often ludicrous attempt to maintain social status and to not be embarrassed.

In everyday life we seldom hear such outlandish excuses. The most common excuse we might hear is "The dog ate my homework." But remember that all of these excuses are an attempt on the part of the complainer to be let off the hook for their poor performance.

Your goal should be to not engage with the excuse someone gives you but, instead, to get the person to commit to doing better in the future. Why? Because they've already failed, and if you try to address their excuse, 1) they will become defensive, and 2) no matter what you say, they will only pile on more excuses.

The magic phrase is to ask simply, "How do you plan to improve next time?" This puts the responsibility back on the complainer and gets them to problem-solve about future incidents.

In summary, here again are the five reasons people complain and how to respond to those complaints.

PURPOSE OF COMPLAINT	RESPONSE
Get attention	"What's going well with . . ."
Remove responsibility	"If it were possible, how might you do it?"
Inspire envy	Compliment them for having the opposite quality of what they're complaining about.
Power	"It sounds like the two of you have a lot to talk about."
Excuse poor performance	"How do you plan to improve next time?"

No complaining!
$100 fine for each
violation.

Browman

Deprived of her favorite means of expression, Kathy was
speechless—much to the relief of her coworkers.

CHAPTER 5

WAKING UP

He who avoids complaint invites happiness.

—ABU BAKR

A young monk entered an order that mandated total silence. At his discretion, the abbot could allow any monk to speak. It was nearly five years before the abbot approached the novice and said, "You may now speak two words."

Choosing his words carefully, the monk said, "Hard bed." With genuine concern the abbot said, "I'm sorry your bed isn't comfortable, we'll see if we can get you another one."

Another half decade passed before the abbot came to the young monk and said, "You may say two more words."

After a few moments' deliberation, the monk said softly, "Cold food."

"We'll see what we can do to serve you hot meals," replied the abbot.

On the monk's fifteenth anniversary, the abbot allowed the monk to again speak two words.

VOICES

I was recently traveling and bad weather had surrounded some of the destination airports, causing many flights to get canceled or delayed. I was sitting by the gate, having changed my flight to another one already, and was watching the unfortunate airline rep at the gate counter. She was being bombarded by a number of people who seemed to assume that the poor weather, flight cancellations, and everything else causing them grief was her fault and each one in turn laid all of their grief on her and I could see she was being pushed to the brink.

A little ah-ha lightbulb flashed in my mind and since I am apt to follow my instinct, I stood up and took my place in the line of people intent on sharing their bad day with her. I patiently waited my turn and when I was finally standing in front of her, her weary eyes looked up to me, her forehead creased with stress, and she asked, "May I help you, sir?"

I said, "Yes you can." I then asked her to act busy while I spoke to her. I told her I stood in line to give her a five-minute break. While she typed (I have no idea what she typed), I explained to her that while all of these people were intent on ruining her day, she had other people in her life that really cared about her and that she had passions in her life that gave her life meaning was far more important than what was happening here today. Given all of that, the stuff happening here wasn't important and shouldn't stress her out. We chatted back and forth for a few minutes as she continued to look busy.

> *After seeing her regain her composure, I knew she had to get back to her work and I wished her a great day, telling her it was time for the next customer. She looked up at me and I could see that her eyes were slightly welling up. "Thank you so much," she said. "I don't know how to thank you for this."*
>
> *I smiled and told her the best way to thank me was to pass on the kindness to someone else when she had the opportunity.*
>
> —HARRY TUCKER
> NEW YORK, NEW YORK

"I quit," said the monk.

"It's probably for the best," replied the abbot with a shrug. "You've done nothing but complain since you got here."

Like the young monk, you probably did not realize how often you complain, but by now you are awakening to the truth about yourself.

We've all experienced sitting, leaning, or lying on one of our arms or legs for a period of time and having it "fall asleep." When we shift our weight and the blood rushes back into the limb, it tingles. Sometimes the tingle is uncomfortable, even painful. The same is true when you begin to wake up to your complaining nature. If you're like most people, realizing how often you complain can be shock-

> "What you are looking for is what is looking."
>
> **—SAINT FRANCIS OF ASSISI**

ing. That's okay. Just keep moving that bracelet and stay with it. Don't allow yourself to give up. Later in this book, I'll devote an entire chapter to the power of commitment, but for now, just remember the incredible power of persistence.

In chapter 2, I mentioned that I was very overweight as a child. In my senior year of high school, I lost in excess of one hundred pounds. When friends asked what diet had achieved such great results, I answered honestly, "The one I stuck with." I had been on dozens of diets but finally stayed with one and trimmed down.

So stick with your commitment to become Complaint Free even when you're shocked and embarrassed by how often you complain. Stick with it when you feel justified in complaining. Stick with it when you crave the opportunity to paint yourself as a victim and gain sympathy from others. Most important, stick with it even when you accumulate several Complaint Free days, stumble, and complain. Even if you're on Day 20, switch your bracelet and start anew. That's all it takes, starting over again and again—moving that bracelet. In the words of Winston Churchill, "Success is stumbling from failure to failure with no loss of enthusiasm."

One of my hobbies is juggling. I learned to juggle from a book that came with three square-shaped bags filled with crushed pecan shells. The bags' shape and contents were designed to keep the bags from rolling away when they were dropped. The implicit message behind the design was: They are *going* to be dropped!

For years I juggled at my daughter's school functions and

other events, but I always decline invitations to juggle at talent shows. Juggling is not a talent; it's a skill. A talent is something you're born with and can be culti-

"The three great essentials to achieve anything worthwhile are, first, hard work; second, stick-to-itiveness; third, common sense."

—THOMAS EDISON

vated and nurtured to full expression, whereas a skill is something most people can learn if they'll only invest enough time.

When I juggle, people will often say, "I wish I could do that."

"You can," I respond. "Just put in the time and stay with it."

"No," they often say, "I'm not coordinated enough." This comment removes from them the responsibility of trying and putting forth any effort.

I've taught several people to juggle, and I always begin by handing them one of the non-rolling bags with an instruction to drop the bag on the floor.

"Now pick it up," I say. My students do.

"Now drop it again." Again, they comply.

"Good! Now pick it up.

"Drop it.

"Pick it up.

"Drop it.

"Pick it up."

We'll go through this many times, until the person begins to tire of the whole exercise and asks, "What does this have to do with learning to juggle?"

"Everything," I say. "If you want to learn to juggle, you

have to be prepared to drop the balls and pick them up hundreds of times. But if you stay with it," I assure the student, "you *can* juggle."

Just keep picking up the balls. Pick them up and start over even when you're tired and frustrated. Pick them up when people laugh at you. Pick them up when it seems like you juggled for a shorter time than the last time before you dropped them. Just keep picking them up.

Every time I've mastered a new juggling maneuver, it has started with dropping and picking up again. The first time I tried to juggle clubs, I spun one club in the air, and its wooden handle smashed hard into my collarbone, raising a painful welt. I threw the clubs in a closet, deciding I could never learn to juggle them.

When they hear about the Complaint Free challenge, many people say, "I wish I could do that, but I can't," even though they've never even tried.

A person who puts their purple bracelet in a drawer is making certain that they will never become Complaint Free. With my clubs collecting dust in the closet, there was no way I'd learn to juggle them. A year later, I hauled them out and tried again.

Being careful to avoid the hard handles as they spun in my direction, I tried to keep three clubs in the air, dropping them repeatedly. However, because I stayed with it I can now juggle not only clubs but also knives and even flaming torches.

Anyone who is willing to pick up the balls, clubs, knives, or torches over and over again can learn to juggle. Anyone willing to

"Complaining about a problem without posing a solution is called whining."

—TEDDY ROOSEVELT

switch their bracelet and start over, and over, and over, can become a Complaint Free person.

You may wonder if what you say is a complaint or a statement of fact. Remember that the difference between a complaint and a statement of fact is the energy you put into your comment. According to Dr. Robin Kowalski, "Whether or not the particular statement reflects a complaint . . . depends on whether the speaker is experiencing an internal dissatisfaction." The words in a complaint and a non-complaint can be identical; what distinguishes the two is your meaning, your energy behind them. The Conscious Incompetent stage is all about becoming aware of what you say and, more important, the energy behind what you're saying.

And relax, there is no prize for being the fastest person to complete the twenty-one-day challenge. In fact, I tend to be skeptical of people who say they have been at it for a week and are already on Day 7. In my experience, these are people who are not aware when they complain. They may have donned the bracelet, but they are still lingering in the Unconscious Incompetence stage.

In my experience, those who are really making progress are like a woman who posted a while back on my Facebook page (www.Facebook.com/WillBowen): "Got my bracelets 10 minutes ago . . . already had to change it around 5 times." An hour later she posted, "I'm up to 10 times!"

I commented simply, "Hang in there, you're on the right track."

Becoming a Complaint Free person is accepting rather than railing against that which cannot be changed.

Thirty years ago, I had a brief but successful career selling life insurance. The first year I worked for the company, I was the ninth-highest-performing salesperson out of nearly a thousand of my peers, and as one of the top performers, I was awarded a trip for two to Europe that included a one-week cruise up the Rhine River followed by a week of sightseeing and shopping in Zurich.

My wife at the time was so excited because this would be her first trip to Europe, and I wanted everything to go perfectly. However, as the saying goes, we make plans and God laughs.

As the two of us flew from Kansas City to New York to connect with our international flight to Germany, the pilot came on the public address system and said that a massive storm was approaching New York. He stated that we would have to go into a holding pattern several hundred miles away from John F. Kennedy International Airport until the bad weather passed. My wife and I looked at each other and our hearts sank, because we had a tight connection to make our flight to Germany.

As our plane flew in a large, lazy circle waiting for the storm

ahead to move on, we repeatedly checked our watches to
see if we would make our
connection. After more than
an hour, it became obvious
that we would not.

"For after all, the best thing one
can do when it is raining is let it
rain."

—HENRY WADSWORTH
LONGFELLOW

"Maybe the international flight was delayed by the storm,"
she said hopefully.

"Maybe," I replied. "I guess we'll just have to wait and see."

When we finally landed at JFK we were disappointed to
discover that our flight to Germany had actually left early to
avoid the storm and we were now stranded. We called the
airline's customer support number and were told that they
could not do anything for us until five A.M.; it was then around
twelve-fifteen A.M.

The airport was filled with similarly grounded travelers all
looking weary and agitated. After walking around the terminal searching for a chair to take a nap in and finding none, we
took off our coats and laid them on the floor, where we managed to get a few hours of uncomfortable sleep.

At four-thirty A.M. we called our tour company and they
informed us that we could not fly into the city we had planned
to because, just like our flight, our ship had already departed.
She said that we would have to meet the ship along its route.
She was very helpful, telling us where to change our flight destination so that we could connect with the rest of our group
already sailing on the Rhine.

Calling the airline to make the arrangements, we were told

that the next available flight to that location left JFK a full seventeen hours later. We made the best of our plight, finally finding a couple of seats, where we napped and waited.

We flew to the city the tour company recommended and then waited an additional three hours for the first of two trains we'd have to take to get to the harbor where the cruise ship was moored for the day. Bleary-eyed from exhaustion, we climbed aboard the first train and rode for several hours. At the proper station, we again waited a couple of hours for the second train, which would take us to the port city where our vessel waited.

Thankfully, the second train trip took only an hour, and at last, we pulled up right in front of the cruise ship. We knew it was our ship because we could see dozens of people wearing tracksuits my company had given us for the trip. As we recognized people from our group, several of them spotted us and rushed over to the train to greet us with excited waves and shouts.

My wife and I gathered our bags and shuffled to the door to exit the train. But the doors didn't open. I pushed the handle and nothing happened. I pushed harder; still nothing. Seeing our struggle, several people began to shout suggestions to us. Unfortunately, they were giving us instructions in German, which neither of us understood.

The shouts outside from our friends ceased. Their fast waves of hello slowly became slow waves of goodbye as the train began to chug, chug, chug, taking us away from our destination. As it turned out, the train's doors had to be opened by stepping on a small pedal, and that's what the helpful Germans had been trying to tell us.

As our cruise ship faded into the distance, we looked at each other in exhausted

> "Life is a series of natural and spontaneous changes. Don't resist them; don't wish things were different. That only creates sorrow. Go along. Let reality be reality."
>
> **—VERNON HOWARD**

bemusement. Arriving in the next town, we managed to get the doors open and stumbled off the train, our luggage in tow. From there we were able to find a taxi with a driver who spoke just enough English to understand our request to return to the port one town back.

We bumped along the cobblestone streets in the rickety old cab for nearly an hour until finally, after nearly three and a half days of travel, we connected with the rest of our tour.

Did we complain? No. We were so grateful to have finally made it that we were overwhelmed with gratitude.

But what if we *had* complained? Would that have changed the weather, prevented our international flight from departing without us, or made our train trips and taxi ride more bearable? No. No amount of complaining would have improved any aspect of our situation. In fact, complaining would have only served to make us both more miserable and upset. And yet we see people do this all the time.

Because of my busy professional speaking schedule, I'm on dozens of flights every year. Statistically, nearly one-third of all flights in the United States are delayed or canceled, and no amount of complaining will change that.

Seven years ago, I flew to Memphis, Tennessee, to deliver a speech at the famous Peabody hotel, where twice each day there is a duck parade. In the morning, a member of the hotel's staff shepherds mallard ducks, which are kept on the hotel's roof, down in the elevator to the lobby, where they waddle along a red carpet and then hop into the hotel fountain. The ducks spend the day splashing about to the delight of guests before returning that evening back along the same red carpet to the elevator and up to the roof.

Glancing around, I spotted a man who had been on my flight from Kansas City to Memphis the day before, and I walked over and struck up a conversation. Our flight had been delayed several hours and we both remarked on how much our fellow passengers had complained about being detained. As it turned out, both he and I traveled a lot for work, and I observed that both he and I had seemed unaffected by the flight delay while some of our fellow passengers had been positively outraged.

He then made a wise observation: "Because you and I travel so frequently, we know how rare it is to have a flight delayed for that long, whereas most of the other travelers rarely fly, so they think this kind of thing happens all the time. As a result, they felt justified in angrily griping about the delay."

Complaining about situations in which we find ourselves does not improve our circumstances. However, complaining does change us, because it makes us less grateful and a lot less happy.

I was recently interviewed by a radio morning show. One

of the hosts said, "But I complain for a living—and I get paid very well for complaining."

"Okay," I said, "and on a scale of one to ten, how happy are you?"

"When he thought to complain about the burden of its weight, he remembered that, because he had the jacket, he had withstood the cold of the dawn."

—PAULO COELHO

After a beat he replied, "Is there a negative number?"

Complaining may benefit us in many ways, such as gaining sympathy and attention—it may even gain us a radio audience—but being happy is not a benefit derived from complaining.

And you deserve to be happy, to have the material possessions you want, to have friendships and relationships that fill your heart and satisfy your desires; you deserve to be healthy and to have a career you enjoy.

Take this in: Anything you desire, you deserve.

Stop making excuses and begin to move toward your dreams. If you are saying things like "Men are commitment-phobic," "Everyone in my family is fat," "I'm not coordinated," or "My high school guidance counselor told me I'd never amount to anything," you are making yourself a victim, and victims never become victors. You alone get to choose which you'll be.

Please know that I get that you may have had some unfortunate and painful things happen to you. Many of us have. You can tell the story about these events forever, be "right" about what happened, and let this be an excuse that limits you your entire life. Or you can be like a slingshot.

What determines how far a stone will fly from a slingshot? The answer is: how far back you've pulled the band. If you study the lives of successful people, you'll find that their success occurred not in spite of their life challenges but often *because* of them. They stopped telling everyone how much they were wronged and began to seek ways of turning the manure of their lives into fertilizer for their growth and success. Their slingshot was pulled back far, and as a result, they soared even farther.

Let your life experiences propel you forward rather than hold you back. Wake up to the beauty that is within you as well as around you. Focus on that, forgive others, let stuff go, and you'll begin to live a happier, healthier, Complaint Free life.

PART 3

CONSCIOUS COMPETENCE

CHAPTER 6

SILENCE AND THE
LANGUAGE OF COMPLAINING

Before you compose a response, compose yourself.

The Conscious Competence stage is one of hypersensitivity. In it, you begin to be aware of everything you say. You are moving your bracelet far less frequently because you are very careful when you speak. You are now talking in more positive terms because you are beginning to catch your words *before* they come out of your mouth. Your purple bracelet has gone from being a tool for recognizing when you complain to being a filter through which your words pass before you speak them.

One family who took the Complaint Free challenge emailed that everyone in the family seemed to hit the Conscious Competence stage at the same time. "For about a week, we just sat at the dinner table and stared at each other afraid to speak," the father told me.

Prolonged periods of silence are typical for a person in the Conscious Competence stage.

VOICES

I got my purple bracelet and was determined to not complain, criticize, or gossip.

I went out to lunch with a friend of mine. When she started talking about things that were "wrong" and wanted me to agree with her, I pulled up my sleeve and showed her my purple bracelet and told her what I was attempting to do.

She said "Well, then, what are we going to talk about?"

That was a very awkward moment. I said, "I don't know." Then I started saying how good the food was that we were eating, and how beautiful the flowers were across the street.

I think I would have been a little put off too, if someone said that to me in the middle of a conversation. But it's getting easier for me, whether I tell my friends/relatives or not. I just change the subject or try to lighten up the conversation. (Or say, "Excuse me, I have to go to the bathroom.")

—JOAN MCCLURE

FORT BRAGG, CALIFORNIA

Before our bracelets were custom-made bearing our Complaint Free World logo, we purchased them from a novelty company that sold them as "spirit" bracelets. If your school color was green, you would order green spirit bracelets, or red spirit bracelets for schools with red as their color, etc.

Once we began to have our bracelets custom-made, we kept the word *spirit* for a while embossed on the side opposite our logo. We did this because *spirit* comes from the Latin *spiritus,* which means "breath." In the Conscious Competence stage, one of the best things you can do is to draw a deep breath

"Smile, breathe and go slowly."

—THÍCH NHẤT HẠNH

rather than speaking out of hand. Complaining is a habit, and taking a moment just to breathe gives you a chance to select your words more carefully. We finally dropped *spirit* from the bracelets because many people saw the word *spirit* and made the understandable assumption that we were somehow instructing people to be religious. A Complaint Free World is a nonreligious human transformation movement.

Spiritus—breath. When you find yourself around other people who are complaining, and you catch yourself feeling compelled to chime in, breathe. When something frustrating happens and you have the chance to unload your frustrations on someone else, breathe.

Breathe. Breathe and remain silent.

Recent research has found that we human beings have two internal pacemakers. One, located in our chest, regulates the rhythm of our heart. The other, which regulates the pace of our breathing, is actually located within our head.

Our mental state and our breathing are so intertwined that, rather than the pacemaker for breathing being located near our lungs, it's in our brain.

If your mind is calm, your breathing is deep and slow. If your mind is racing, your breathing becomes shallow and rapid.

You can slow your breathing by calming your mind, and

you can also calm your mind by slowing your breathing. Yogis have been trying to teach us this for millennia.

Stephen Elliott, author of *The New Science of Breath,* has discovered that if you can inhale for a count of 5.8 seconds and then exhale for 5.8 seconds, you match the ideal rate for resetting your breathing pacemaker, and as a result, you calm your mind.

Elliott has created a recording called "2 Bells" under the name Coherence that does just that. You can find the song on Amazon Music, Apple Music, and Spotify, as well as most other music platforms, and this is what I use in my meditation practice every day. Simply inhale along with the sound of the higher bell and then exhale along with the lower bell. Doing this before you even get out of bed will cause your breathing to become slow, deep, and rhythmic, and your mind will be calm and free of stress for hours.

If you're a person who likes to pray, the Conscious Competence stage is a good time to deepen your prayer life. You've reached a point where you really don't want to move your bracelet, so take a breath, and in that moment of silence say a little prayer before speaking. Ask for guidance so that your words will be constructive rather than destructive. And if no words come, remain silent. It's better to remain silent than to complain and have to start the twenty-one-day challenge over on Day 1.

Back when I was a young man selling radio advertising, I worked with a guy who talked infrequently, if at all. After getting to know him, I asked why he sat without talking in meetings while others droned on incessantly. He replied, "If I'm quiet, people assume that I'm smarter than I am." If you simply say nothing, people may at least give you

"Even a fool, when he holdeth his peace, is counted wise: and he that shutteth his lips is esteemed a man of understanding."

—PROVERBS 17:28

credit for being smart. When we run off at the mouth, we don't make ourselves sound intelligent, we simply say that we're not comfortable enough with ourselves to let quiet reign, if even for a moment.

One of the ways we know we've met a person who is special to us is that we can be with them with no words being spoken. We're simply comfortable in their presence and enjoy their company, and a lot of mindless jabbering doesn't improve our time with them, it makes it less precious.

Silence allows you to reflect and to carefully select your words, to speak of things you wish to put your creative energy toward rather than allowing your discomfort to cause you to spout off a laundry list of grievances.

This stage of becoming Complaint Free was described in an email we received from a lieutenant colonel at the Pentagon:

A quick update on how we're doing. All twelve bracelets are distributed among my co-workers, and so far there is one gal (who has always been quiet and low-key) who is having some great success. I think she actually got into double digits!

The rest of us, however, are finding it more difficult

than we even imagined. It HAS done something very important for us, though . . . when we are complaining, we know about it, we pause, we move our bracelets, and we restate what we were saying more positively. I haven't even gone an entire day yet, but I can see what a powerful communication tool it is for the synergy of an office. We are able to laugh at ourselves when we're complaining and challenge each other to find a better way. I'll send another update when someone reaches their goal. (Everyone is excited about expanding the challenge to more folks here in the Pentagon, so we're moving forward.)

HAVE A GREAT AIR FORCE DAY!
—CATHY HAVERSTOCK

I can remember the first time I decided to watch what I said very carefully, knowing that it was a reflection of my thoughts and that my thoughts create my reality. I borrowed a twenty-year-old pickup truck to retrieve some things I had in storage. This old F-150 had several hundred thousand miles on its original engine and got about twenty miles to the gallon—of oil! I had to stop repeatedly to add oil, and I even carried a case of thirty-weight in the truck bed.

As I left to retrieve my belongings, a trip of a hundred-plus miles, I made sure the oil reservoir was filled and invited my dog Gibson to ride in the cab to keep me company.

It took several hours to drive from my home in Aynor,

South Carolina, to the storage unit in Manning, South Carolina, adding oil multiple times along the way.

> "You have to believe. Otherwise, it will never happen."
>
> **—NEIL GAIMAN**

As Gibson and I drove back, I decided to take a shortcut and headed down a dark two-lane country road toward Greeleyville, South Carolina. I used to live in Manning and knew the route well. In fact, I used to ride my bike to Greeleyville and back on weekends for exercise because it was a stretch of about thirteen miles one-way with little traffic and even fewer homes.

I had been meticulously checking and adding oil to the old truck all day, but as the sun began to set, the CHECK ENGINE light came on. As was my habit, my mind went to "Oh, no! I'm in trouble! I'm way out here in the middle of nowhere." But I caught myself. I remembered my commitment to monitor and control my thoughts and words.

I turned to Gibson, who lay dozing on the seat next to me, and said, "This is going to work out perfectly, buddy." Honestly, I thought I was a little crazy. Not for talking to a dog, but for thinking that I would somehow make it home in this dilapidated old truck dripping oil while driving down deserted country roads. As I said, I knew this stretch of road well. In the thirteen miles there were only a dozen or so homes scattered sporadically along the road, and I was not carrying a cell phone.

The truck sputtered and spat but continued on for about a mile, until suddenly the engine died. Through gritted teeth I said, "This is going to work out fine," attempting to convince myself as the truck began to slow and finally glide to a stop directly in front of someone's home.

"What luck!" I said to both myself and to Gibson, celebrating the moment and yet still amazed at how fortunate we had been. "Maybe the people who live here are at home and they'll let me use their phone." I reasoned that I could call someone to come and pick us up, and leave the truck at the side of the road until I could have it repaired.

Then I remembered the truck bed loaded with my belongings and said aloud, "No. I would rather be able to drive home tonight and not have to leave my stuff on the side of the road. I don't know how this is going to work out, but I'm going to believe that it is. I see myself parked in my driveway, tonight, in this truck with all my possessions."

Now, remember, this was *not* my typical way of thinking. In the past, I would have gotten out of the truck and probably done something helpful like swear or kick one of its tires. Instead, I closed my eyes and visualized Gibson and me pulling into our driveway. In my mental picture, it was evening— just as it was at that time—and I was in the same clothes I was currently wearing. I allowed myself to sit a moment and clearly take this image in before walking up the long driveway and ringing the doorbell.

I heard people stirring inside the house. I smiled and said aloud, "Unbelievable! The only house for miles and people are home just at the moment my truck breaks down." A man answered, and we exchanged introductions. I explained about the truck and asked if I might use his phone; he peered past me into the darkness and asked, "What kind of truck are you driving?"

"Believe as a child believes and the magic will find you."

—TERESA LANGDON

"A Ford," I said.

He smiled. "Well, I'm the service manager at the Ford truck dealership. Let me get my tools and take a look."

I was positively giddy with excitement. Not only had our truck broken down directly in front of someone's house on a desolate stretch of road, but the man who lived there was responsible for all the repairs for a hundred miles or more on trucks of the very make I was driving!

I held a flashlight for him as the man tinkered under the hood for about fifteen minutes. He finally turned and said, "The problem is that there is something wrong with your fuel system. You need a small part. Doesn't cost but a dollar or two, but I don't have one here at my house and the dealership is closed.

"What you've got," he continued, "is more of a plumbing problem than a mechanical problem."

"That's okay," I said with a shrug. "Maybe I can just use your phone, then?"

"Well," he said, "you've got a plumbing problem, and my dad's visiting from Kentucky. He's a plumber. Let me go get him."

As the man trotted back to the house to retrieve his father, I scrubbed the fur on Gibson's neck, smiling deliriously.

A few minutes later the man's father had diagnosed the truck's problem.

"You need a piece of tubing about two inches long and one-quarter inch wide," he said.

"Like this one?" his son said, drawing the exact size tube we needed from his toolbox.

"Yes, that's it!" said the father. "Where did you find one?"

"I don't know where it came from," his son said. "I found it on my workbench a month or so ago and just dropped it in the toolbox in case I ever needed it."

Five minutes later Gibson and I were back on the road. "What an experience," I said to Gibson, who was now excitedly poking his nose out of the passenger window.

It *had* worked out. We were on our way. I would be pulling into the driveway that very night with my belongings.

But at that precise moment the OIL light lit up the dash. We had sat for so long in front of the man's home that the oil had drained from the truck, and it was dangerously low. Before leaving the storage unit, I had poured the last quart I had into the oil reserve.

Seeing no homes ahead, I began to get concerned but then stopped myself, saying loudly, "It worked once, it will work again!" As I drove, I again conjured up the image of us pulling safely into our driveway that very night.

Turning the corner into the tiny town of Greeleyville, I pulled into the only gas station in town. The owner was just locking the door for the night.

"Can I help you?" he asked.

"I need oil," I said.

Switching the station lights back on, he said, "Get

> "The moment you doubt whether you can fly, you cease forever to be able to do it."
>
> —J. M. BARRIE

what you need." As I walked toward the shelf that held the quarts of oil, I shoved my hands into my pants pockets and pulled out all the money I was carrying. At the rate the truck was dropping oil, I knew I might need at least four quarts just to make it home. Quickly counting my money, I realized that I had only $4.56 with me. I grabbed two quarts, which was all I could afford, and laid them on the counter.

"Did you see the other brand?" the owner asked.

"No," I said.

He began walking toward the shelves, and I followed.

"There!" he said. "It's a good brand, better I think than the one you picked out, but I'm not going to carry it anymore so we just put it on sale today—half-price." Happy to the point of elation but not wanting to seem mentally unbalanced, I swept four quarts of the oil up into my arms and walked briskly to the counter. At 11:17 that very night, I pulled the truck into our driveway.

How did that happen? What celestial maneuverings took place? What realignment of possibilities and probabilities transpired to facilitate this miracle? And how in the world did it work?

The answer is that I had faith and did not complain to myself, or even Gibson, about what we were going through. The future is not set, and to complain about present circumstances only serves to carry undesirable conditions forward.

One of the questions I'm often asked is "But don't you need to complain to get what you want?" As we discussed previously with the DEARMAN strategy, you can get what you desire best by expressing what you want rather than complaining about how you don't want things to be.

The shortest path to get what you desire is to not talk about or focus on the problem. Focus *beyond* the problem. Only talk about what you desire, and only to someone who can provide the solution. You will shorten the wait time for what you seek, and be happier in the process.

"But every great thing in our country began with people complaining. Think about Thomas Jefferson and Martin Luther King!" an email I received stated.

I realized that in one respect I agreed with the woman who sent the email. The first step toward progress is dissatisfaction. But if we stay in dissatisfaction, we never move forward. And those who complain as a matter of course chart their destination to be the same unhappy port from which they sailed. Our focus must be on what we want to occur rather than what we do not.

Jefferson and King both pointed out our nation's dissatisfaction with prevailing conditions, but they did not leave it there. They painted a picture of what could be. Their dissatisfaction drove them to envision the predominant challenges fully resolved, and their passion for these visions inspired

others to follow. Their relentless focus on a bright
future made the collective
heart of the nation race.
They lived the words of
George Bernard Shaw, who

"Instead of wasting your time
complaining focus on the
opportunities that can change the
situation."

—NITIN NAMDEO

wrote, "You see things; and you say 'Why?' But I dream things
that never were; and I say 'Why not?'"

Complainers ask, "Why?"

Complaint Free people ask, "Why not?"

On August 28, 1963, more than two hundred thousand
Americans marched on Washington demanding equal rights
for all. At this historic event, Reverend Dr. Martin Luther King,
Jr., stood on the steps of the Lincoln Memorial, his words cast-
ing a spell over the assembled mass. King identified the problem. He said, "America has given the Negro people a bad check,
a check which has come back marked 'insufficient funds.'"
But he did not leave his audience drowning in his words of
dissatisfaction. Rather, he inspired them to hope with a vision
of a world yet to come.

King declared, "I have a dream!" And he then delivered what
the website American Rhetoric named "the greatest speech of
the twentieth century." King constructed in the minds of his
listeners a world without racism. He said that he had "been to
the mountaintop," and his words carried us there with him.
Dr. King focused beyond the problem at hand on the resolution
sought.

In the Declaration of Independence, Thomas Jefferson

clearly stated the challenges the colonies were having under the governance of the British Empire. However, this document was not just a litany of gripes. Had it been, it probably would not have fired the imagination of the world and unified the colonies.

The first paragraph of the U.S. Declaration of Independence reads:

> *When in the Course of human events, it becomes necessary for one people to dissolve the political bands which have connected them with another, and to assume among the powers of the earth, the separate and equal station to which the Laws of Nature and of Nature's God entitle them . . .*

For a moment, imagine you are a citizen of one of the original thirteen colonies and you read those words, "the separate and *equal* station to which the Laws of Nature and of Nature's God entitle them." At the time Jefferson wrote this, the British Empire was the world's greatest superpower, and Jefferson stated without hyperbole that this fledgling and diverse band of colonies was "equal" to this political and military behemoth.

Consider the collective gasp this inspired among the colonists, followed by the resulting swell of pride and optimism. How could they ever aspire to such a lofty ideal as to be equal to Britain? Because "the Laws of Nature and of Nature's God entitle[d] them."

This was not complaining, this was a compelling vision

for a bright future. This was focusing beyond the problems at hand on a resolution sought.

"The most important thing to remember is this: to be ready at any moment to give up what you are for what you might become."

—W.E.B. DU BOIS

You, too, have a bright future ahead if you'll just stop complaining. Change the words you use and watch your life change. For example:

INSTEAD OF	CONSIDER
problem	opportunity
setback	challenge
tormentor	mentor
pain	discomfort
I insist	I would like
I have to	I get to
complaint	request
struggle	journey

Give it a try. It may feel awkward as you begin, but watch how changing your words also changes your attitude about a person or situation. As your words change, your perspective about things will also change.

One of the more common questions I'm asked is some variation of "If I drop something on my foot and I curse, is that a complaint?"

The answer is no. This is, believe it or not, a natural reflex.

Now, before you think I'm suggesting that you begin swearing like a character in a Quentin Tarantino movie, let me explain. Curse words are actually stored in a different part of your brain than other words you use in everyday language. It's as if swear words are just below the surface and ready for you to employ them without even having to think what to say when something upsetting happens. You experience an upsetting cause, and the effect is the utterance (even the shouting) of a curse that you typically use in such situations.

The interesting thing is that you select your own curse words over time and they get lodged in that part of your brain, available for immediate access when needed.

Yesterday, my neighbor was helping me install an anchor cleat on my boat. He was working in the hot sun, sweat pouring down his face, and his body was contorted into an uncomfortable position inside the anchor well. Blood rose on his arms from dozens of thin cuts he received from the sharp pieces of fiberglass he was trying to work around.

Suddenly, a nut and washer slipped out of his sweaty hand and both clinked, clanged, and then tumbled deep into the bowels of the boat's hull. My neighbor is a super-chill guy, and even though I'm sure he was very frustrated, he just let out a sigh and began looking for the fallen parts.

No sooner had he retrieved them and begun to put them into place than he dropped them again, and this time he said, "Ahh . . . FUDGE!" Given the circumstances and his frustration, that was not the particular F-word I expected. But his reaction reminded me that we all choose our own curse words, and once we have made our selection, they get stored in that little curse bin in our brain, ready to pop out when we're upset. He had made a conscious choice at some point that "Fudge!" was the depth of his profanity, and so that's what he said.

> "Vulgarity is like a fine wine: it should only be uncorked on a special occasion, and then only shared with the right group of people."
>
> **—JAMES ROZOFF**

Now, consider this. Given the looping nature of our words and our emotions, I have observed that people who use profane curses frequently tend to be more easily upset than those who do not. In other words, I believe it's not that volatile people curse, I believe the act of cursing actually triggers being upset in the mind of the person using the profanity. If you find you're easily upset, one thing you might consider is not using curse words in everyday conversation and you'll probably find that you're less easily upset and happier overall.

In the introduction to this book, I mentioned that the average person complains fifteen to thirty times a day. As you're taking the Complaint Free challenge, you'll soon discover whether you're below or above average when it comes to how often you complain. And if you find yourself struggling, it could be because of the environment in which you were raised.

You might find it both interesting and helpful to take the following Revised Lifestyle Orientation Test (LOT-R) to see if you are more naturally optimistic or pessimistic[1]:

Honestly respond to each of the following statements using these numbers:

| 0 | Strongly Disagree
| 1 | Disagree
| 2 | Neutral
| 3 | Agree
| 4 | Strongly Agree

*** Remember to be honest, there are no right or wrong answers. ***

	STATEMENT	RESPONSE
1	In uncertain times, I usually expect the best.	
2	It's easy for me to relax.	
3	If something can go wrong for me, it will.	
4	I'm always optimistic about my future.	
5	I enjoy my friends a lot.	
6	It's important for me to keep busy.	
7	I hardly ever expect things to go my way.	
8	I don't get upset too easily.	
9	I rarely count on good things happening to me.	
10	Overall, I expect more good things to happen to me than bad.	

SCORING

1. Ignore your scores for statements 2, 5, 6, and 8. These are just filler statements.

2. Before you figure out your overall score, REVERSE the scores you gave for statements 3, 7, and 9. This means that (0 = 4), (1 = 3), (2 = 2), (3 = 1), and (4 = 0).

3. After you have reversed your scores for statements 3, 7, and 9, total your scores for statements 1, 3, 4, 7, 9, and 10.

SCORE RANGE	INTERPRETATION
0–13	Low optimism (high pessimism)
14–18	Moderate optimism
19–24	High optimism (low pessimism)

Regardless of where you fall on the optimism vs. pessimism spectrum, you can increase your score by becoming a Complaint Free person. If you can't say anything nice, practice silence and don't say anything at all. If you do say something, make sure it's not a complaint.

CHAPTER 7

CRITICISM AND SARCASM

Sarcasm I now see to be, in general, the language of the devil;
for which reason I have long since as good as renounced it.
—THOMAS CARLYLE

Both criticism and sarcasm are forms of complaining. When you engage in either, switch your bracelet.

Criticism is defined as pointing out another's faults in a disapproving way. Therefore, "constructive criticism" is an oxymoron. To be constructive is to build up. To criticize is to tear down. You are never being constructive when you criticize someone.

No one likes to be criticized. And criticism is ineffective as a strategy because it often increases rather than diminishes the behavior you dislike.

Great leaders know that people respond much more favorably to appreciation than to criticism. Appreciation inspires a person to excel, so as to receive more appreciation. Criticism tears people down, and those who don't feel worthwhile don't feel they can do a good job.

A vicious cycle is created. A person makes a mistake and

> **VOICES**
>
> *I was doing very well with becoming Complaint Free. I had strung a series of days together and could tell it was changing my life.*
>
> *My husband insisted that I stop. He said I was simply not as much fun to be around. I guess he thinks complaining is fun and I wouldn't join in with him and his griping anymore.*
>
> *This makes me sad.*
>
> —NAME WITHHELD

the boss criticizes. The employee feels inadequate and makes another mistake, which the boss also criticizes. This leads to more mistakes, followed by criticisms, followed by more mistakes.

The key is to talk not about what the person didn't do in the past, but rather about what you want the person to do in the future. Instead of "You didn't turn in your time card by five P.M. again! What are you, stupid?" consider "Time cards are due at five P.M., thanks for remembering so I don't have to bug you about it."

Criticism is an attack. And when people are attacked, they have two options: stand and fight, or run away. They may not fight, but just because they withdraw, don't think the war is over. They will continue this or other annoying behavior as a means of counterattacking. All people seek power, and if the only way to acquire it is through passive-aggressive behavior, they'll behave passive-aggressively.

Attention drives behavior. As much as we'd like to feel it's the other way around, it's not true. When we criticize someone, we

"People ask you for criticism, but they only want praise."

—W. SOMERSET MAUGHAM

are inviting future demonstrations of what we are criticizing. This is true for your spouse, your children, your employees, and your friends. In George Bernard Shaw's play *Pygmalion*, Eliza Doolittle explains this phenomenon to Colonel Pickering: "You see, really and truly, apart from the things anyone can pick up (the dressing and the proper way of speaking, and so on), the difference between a lady and a flower girl is not how she behaves, but how she's treated. I shall always be a flower girl to Professor Higgins, because he always treats me as a flower girl, and always will; but I know I can be a lady to you, because you always treat me as a lady, and always will."

We are far more powerful in the creation of our lives than we realize. Our thoughts about people determine how they will show up for us and how we will relate to them. Our words let others know our expectations of them and their behavior. If the words are critical, then the behavior will mirror the expectation represented by what we say.

We all know of parents who focus on a child's poor marks rather than celebrating the child's good grades. The child brings home a report card with four A's and one C, and the parent says, "Why did you get a C?" The focus is on the one average grade rather than on the four excellent ones.

My own daughter, Lia, who had always had excellent

grades, began to let her schoolwork slip at one point. When she brought home her report card, I celebrated the A's and B's and said nothing about the lower grades.

"Aren't you angry about the bad grades?" she asked.

"Why should I be angry?" I said. "They're your grades. If you're happy with them, then that's all that matters."

She wasn't happy with them, and in a very short time she brought them all up. If I had berated her for her low grades, she might have felt disempowered and angry and could have let all of her grades slip farther just to be recalcitrant. When I gave her the authority to decide if her grades were acceptable, she made choices that were actually beyond what I would have encouraged her to aspire to.

Leadership can be a daunting task. The use of criticism is an indication of a leader who lacks the resources to truly lead.

A leader's job is to inspire people to reach their highest level of performance. When someone does their best, the organization benefits and the person experiences the satisfaction of accomplishment. The employee feels the thrill of calling forth hidden resources they never knew existed. People grow when they reach deep and do more, and this is both exciting and stimulating for them.

A leader's job is the careful balancing of inspiration and direction.

A while back, I was speaking at a conference, and before my speech I chatted with the CEO of the sponsoring company. He had grown his business from a simple idea to a multinational, multimillion-dollar-a-year company in just a decade. As we spoke, he told me about his company's phenomenal growth and shared what had become his greatest challenge.

"For a long time, my employees hated me," he said. "I got things done, sure, but I left people's feelings scorched by my criticisms. Our explosive growth began to plateau and then to decline."

"What did you do?" I asked.

"I had to learn to inspire people without killing their spirit," he said. "I took a trip out west just to get away, and quite by accident I learned a powerful lesson."

"What was that?" I asked.

"I took part in a cattle drive," he said. "My job was to keep the cows moving, but I found that there's a fine line between advancing the cows and scattering the herd. After one day pushing the cows so hard that I nearly caused a stampede, I finally asked an old-time cowboy what I was doing wrong.

"He told me that before a cow moves, it shifts its weight in the direction it plans to go. He said I should not push the cows until they moved. Just nudge them until I saw their weight shift in the direction I wanted them to go. As soon as I saw them shift their weight, I should back off."

The CEO continued, "It's a real skill to know how much

pressure to apply to get the cows to shift in a certain direction, and then to back off. Often I pushed too hard and a few times not hard enough, but eventually I figured it out.

"I realized that leading people is not unlike herding cows," he said. "When I inspire them to move a certain way, and they start to shift in that direction, I then need to back off. What I used to do was, rather than backing off, I would feel I needed to goad them to keep going. I would explain my reasons and stress the importance of moving in that direction. Even though they were going where I wanted, I pushed them out of fear they might stop. As a result, they would slow their pace and I'd criticize.

"Then they would feel disempowered and resent me," he said. "And they'd become less, not more, inclined to move. So now as soon as I see my people starting to go the way I want, I ease off and they continue in that direction."

Recently, I listened to a podcast about the difference between managers who are harsh and critical, and those who are encouraging and empowering. Ironically, both approaches work at getting the job done, with one glaring exception. Critical managers get the tasks accomplished but they pay the price of much higher employee turnover. And as most companies know, it's much less expensive to maintain employees than to find, interview, hire, and train new ones.

In *Business Stripped Bare,* Sir Richard Branson writes that the key to management is to know that deep down people want to do what is best for themselves and for the organiza-

tion. He writes that all people are universally hard on
themselves. A leader who
understands this will know

"The employer usually gets the
employees he deserves."

—J. PAUL GETTY

that even without criticism, good people will stop themselves
from repeating mistakes.

For a leader in a family, civic group, church, or business,
greatness lies in learning to urge people only until they show
a subtle shift toward the direction in which you wish them to
go, and then to back off. This movement builds pride, which
fuels momentum.

Like criticism, sarcasm is also complaining. Criticism is
a complaint wielded as a direct attack, whereas sarcasm is
passive-aggressive complaining.

In the movie *Sling Blade*, country music star turned actor
Dwight Yoakam plays an angry young man named Doyle.
Doyle repeatedly says mean, hurtful, and even vicious things
to the other characters and then waves away his cutting re-
marks with a snarky "Hey, I'm just kidding."

A sarcastic person is a hit-and-run driver making a negative statement and then shouting over their shoulder as they
speed off, "Hey, I was just kidding!"

The definition of *sarcasm* is "a sharp and often satirical or
ironic utterance designed to cut or give pain; a cutting, often
ironic remark intended to wound." Researching the etymology
explains the cutting nature of sarcasm. The Greek root of *sarcasm* is *sarkazein*, which means "ripping or tearing away of

the flesh." *Sarkazein* was a form of torture used in ancient medieval times.

For some reason, sarcasm has become chic these days. You'll often see people with just the word *Sarcastic* on their T-shirt, and sarcasm is even listed proudly on people's dating app profiles. It has, somehow, become culturally "cute," for some, to be sarcastic. But sarcasm is anything but cute. Today's sarcasm may not tear people's skin but it certainly tears down their sense of worth.

As I was taking the twenty-one-day challenge, by far the hardest thing for me was to stop being sarcastic.

People ask, "What's wrong with a little sarcasm? I'm just being funny." Sarcasm is always a critical statement with a funny spin. Sarcasm is a cutting remark couched in the plausible deniability of telling a joke. It's the last emotional hiding place of a person who wants to make a point but who does not want to be held responsible for any fallout that may occur as a result.

When I and my group were in Tanzania helping to build a birthing center for a nonprofit hospital, we took an afternoon off to visit a museum of African artifacts. We piled into an old van for a bouncy journey along the dirt roads of Mwanza, dodging large boulders, some big as bathtubs, which festooned our path. Our driver had to make wide swerves to avoid them.

I was seated next to a young man who was translating my conversation with our guide into Swahili. After we had swerved wide to the left and then back to the right to avoid one especially large boulder, I leaned toward our guide and said sarcastically, "Wow, nice roads."

"Employee loyalty is cheaper than hiring new employees, training them, and motivating them."

—POOJA AGNIHOTRI

Our translator remained silent.

"Aren't you going to translate what I said?" I asked.

"I can't," he replied.

"Why not?" I inquired.

"Because what you said was sarcastic, and the African people do not understand sarcasm. If I tell him that you said the roads are nice, he will believe you. If I tell him you don't like the roads, it sounds critical."

"People here don't ever speak sarcastically?" I asked.

"No, we don't have a word for sarcasm. We have no understanding of saying something and meaning its opposite," he said. "To us you say only what you mean."

Perhaps there is no connection between the upbeat demeanor of the people there and a lack of sarcasm. But maybe there is peace that comes from knowing that when someone says something, they mean it.

Incidentally, and this I believe correlates directly to their overall happiness, people in Africa consider it rude to complain to others. They think that taking your burden and placing it on another's shoulders does not lessen your unhappiness but adds it to the listener.

Criticism and sarcasm are two of the most insidious forms of complaining. Watch how often you criticize or make a sarcastic remark, and when you do, switch your bracelet. Start back over on Day 1.

And remember . . .

There is no shame in Day 1!

"Sarcasm is the last refuge of the imaginatively bankrupt."

—CASSANDRA CLARE

CHAPTER 8

HONK IF YOU'RE HAPPY

Happiness is when what you think,
what you say, and what you do are in harmony.

—GANDHI

The Conscious Competence step is what many people have called the "I'm not going to move my bracelet" stage. You begin to say something, and realizing you are about to complain, gossip, criticize, or express sarcasm, you catch yourself and say instead, "And I'm not going to move my bracelet."

Many have found it helpful during the twenty-one-day challenge to get a "Complaint Free buddy," an accountability partner to help them stay with the challenge and be honest about their progress.

This accountability and the support of other people have proven so valuable to helping people succeed with the challenge that I've created a members-only program called the Complaint Free Life Inner Circle, which provides videos, audio recordings, weekly webinars, and daily accountability.

Check it out at www.ComplaintFreeLife.com.

As I mentioned in chapter 1, one of the most common side

VOICES

I have been working on going complaint free and it is rubbing off on my family.

My daughter Rose is a sixth grader with all the typical drama of adolescent girls.

One of her "friends" wrote her a note stating that Rose was a terrible friend and listed a lot of reasons. It also stated that all the other girls in their clique feel the same way.

When Rose told me this story, I was really nervous because this is a big deal in the life of a sixth grader. I asked her what she did.

Rose said she told the girl, "I'm going to pretend I never got that letter. From now on let's only say nice things to each other. I really like your shoes."

The other girl was so surprised that she just started laughing.

I'm so proud of my girl and I really think my bracelet and my explaining to Rose how I am not complaining has paid off.

—RACHEL KAMINER

WHITE PLAINS, NEW YORK

effects of becoming Complaint Free is an increased feeling of happiness. As you cease griping about the problems in your life and begin to talk about what is going well, your mind cannot help but respond to this new focus.

About twelve years ago, I met a man who helped someone

he dearly loved reframe what seemed to be a hopelessly negative, even tragic, situation.

It all started with a little sign.

The sign was made from a tattered piece of cardboard stapled to what looked like one of those sticks given away at hardware stores to stir paint. Thirty years ago, as I was about to drive across the causeway over the Waccamaw River, just outside Conway, South Carolina, I noticed the sign one day. There, along the side of the road, shoved into the ground amid the litter and the fire ant beds, it said simply,

Honk If
You're Happy

I shook my head at the naïveté of the sign's creator and continued driving, my horn silent.

"What a bunch of fluff!" I snorted to myself. "Happy? What is happiness?" I'd never really known happiness. I'd known pleasure. But even in my moments of greatest pleasure and fulfillment, I found myself wondering when something bad was going to happen to bring me back to reality. "Happy is a scam. Life is painful and challenging, and if things are going well, there is something around the next corner that is going to snap you out of the happy fantasy really fast. Maybe you're happy after you die," I thought, but I wasn't even sure about that.

A couple of weeks later my daughter, Lia, then age three, and I were riding in

"No man is happy who does not think himself so."

—PUBLILIUS SYRUS

the car down Highway 544 toward Surfside Beach to see some friends. We were singing along to a cassette called *Favorite Kids' Songs*, laughing and enjoying our time together. As we neared the causeway to cross the Waccamaw River, I saw the sign again and, without thinking, tapped my horn.

"What?" asked Lia, wondering if perhaps there was something in the road.

"There's this sign on the side of the road that says, HONK IF YOU'RE HAPPY," I replied. "I feel happy so I honked."

The sign made perfect sense to Lia. Children don't have concepts of time, taxing responsibilities, disappointment, betrayal, or any of the other constraints or wounds that adults carry. To her, life was in the moment, and every moment was meant for happiness.

Later that day, as we made our way home back across the bridge and passed the sign again, Lia shrieked, "Honk the horn, Daddy, honk the horn!" By this time, my perspective had shifted. Earlier that day, I'd been looking forward to time with friends; now I was thinking of the many pressing and stressful things that awaited me at work the following day. My mood was anything but happy, but I still tapped the horn to appease my daughter.

What happened next, I'll never forget. Deep inside and just for a moment, I noticed that I felt a little happier than I had just seconds before—as if honking the horn made me happier. Perhaps it was some sort of Pavlovian response. Maybe hearing the horn caused me to conjure up some of the good feelings I'd had when I'd honked that morning.

From that point on, we could not pass that particular stretch of highway without Lia reminding me to honk. I noticed that each time I did, my emotional thermostat rose. If on a one-to-ten scale I was feeling an emotional two, when I honked the horn my happiness grew to a six or seven. I noticed this happened each time we passed the sign and I honked the horn. Soon, I began to honk as I passed the sign even when I was alone in the car.

> "Happiness cannot be traveled to, owned, earned, worn, or consumed. Happiness is the spiritual experience of living every minute with love, grace, and gratitude."
>
> **—DENIS WAITLEY**

The positive feeling I had when I honked at the sign began to extend. I found myself looking forward to that particular section of road, and even before I reached the sign, I noticed I began to feel happier inside. In time, when I turned onto Highway 544, I noticed that my happiness set point would immediately begin to rise. That entire 13.4-mile stretch began to become a place of emotional rejuvenation for me.

The sign was on the shoulder of the highway, in front of some woods that separated nearby homes from the causeway. I found myself wondering who put the sign up and for what purpose.

At that time in my life, I was selling life insurance to people in their homes. One afternoon, I had an appointment to meet with a family who lived about a mile north of Highway 544, but when I arrived the mother told me that her husband had forgotten our meeting and we would need to reschedule. For a moment, I felt dejected, but as I was driving out of the housing development, I realized that I was on the back side of the woods that bordered the highway. As I drove along the road, I estimated where I was in relation to the HONK IF YOU'RE HAPPY sign and when I felt I was close, I stopped at the nearest home.

The house was a one-story, gray manufactured home with dark red trim. As I climbed the cinnamon stairs to the front deck, I noticed that the home was simple but well maintained.

I began to mentally prepare what I would say if someone answered the door. I considered "Hi, I saw a cardboard sign on the highway on the other side of those woods and was wondering if you know anything about it." Or maybe even "Excuse me, but are you the 'Honk If You're Happy' people?"

I felt awkward, but I wanted to know more about the sign that had had such an impact on my thinking and my life. After I rang the doorbell, I didn't get a chance to say any of the lines I had rehearsed.

"Come in!" a man said with a broad, warm smile.

Now I really felt awkward. I thought, "He must be expecting someone else and thinks I'm that person." I entered the home and he enthusiastically shook my hand. I explained that I had driven the highway near his home for more than a year and had seen a sign that said, HONK IF YOU'RE HAPPY. By my estimation, his house was the one closest to the sign and I wondered if he knew anything about it. He smiled and told me that he had put the sign up. Further, he told me that I was not the first person to stop in to inquire about it.

As I heard a couple of horn blasts from a car in the near distance, he explained, "I'm a coach at the local high school. My wife and I enjoy living here near the beach and we love the

"I have learned from experience that the greater part of our happiness or misery depends on our dispositions and not on our circumstances."

—MARTHA WASHINGTON

people. We've been happy together for many years." His clear blue eyes seemed to penetrate mine. "A while back," he said, "my wife got sick. The doctors told us there was nothing they could do. They told her to get her affairs in order and said she had about four months to live, six months at the outside."

I was uncomfortable with the brief silence that followed, but he wasn't. "First we were in shock," he said. "Then we got angry. Then we held each other and cried for what seemed like days. Finally, we accepted that her life would be ending soon. She prepared herself for death. We moved a hospital bed into our room, and she lay there in the dark. We were both miserable.

"One day I was sitting on the deck while she tried to sleep," he continued. "She was in so much pain; it was hard for her to doze off. I was drowning in despair. My heart ached. And yet as I sat there, I could hear the cars crossing the causeway to go to the beach." His eyes drifted up to the corner of the room as he thought about that moment. Then, remembering he was talking to someone, he shook his head, returned his gaze to me, and picked up the story. "Did you know that the Grand

Strand—what people call the sixty miles of beach along South Carolina's coast—is one of the top tourist destinations in the United States?"

Um . . . yes, I do know that," I said. "More than thirteen million tourists come here to vacation every year."

"That's right," he said. "And have you ever been happier than when you're going on vacation? You plan, you save, and then you go off to enjoy some time with your family. It's great!"

A long honk off in the distance punctuated his statement.

The coach thought for a moment and then continued, "It hit me as I sat there on the deck that although my wife was dying, happiness didn't have to die with her. In fact, happiness was all around us. It was riding by in the cars that passed just a few hundred feet from our house every day. So I put up the sign. I didn't have any expectations for it; I just wanted the people in their cars not to take this moment for granted. This special, never-again-to-be-repeated moment with the ones they care for most should be savored, and they should be *aware* of their happiness in the moment."

Several honks sounded from different horns in rapid succession. "My wife began to hear the honks," he said. "Just a few here and there at first. She asked me if I knew anything about it and I told her about the sign. In time, the number of cars honking began to grow and they became like medicine for her. As she lay there, she heard the horns and found great comfort in knowing that she was not isolated in a dark room dying. She was part of the happiness of the world. It was literally all around her."

I sat for a moment, trying to take in what the coach had shared. What a touching and inspiring story.

"Would you like to meet her?" he asked.

"Uh . . . yes," I said with some surprise. We'd spoken

> "Man is fond of counting his troubles, but he does not count his joys. If he counted them up as he ought to, he would see that every lot has enough happiness provided for it."
>
> —FYODOR DOSTOYEVSKY

for so long about his wife that I'd begun to think of her more as a character in a rich and wonderful story than as a real person. As we walked down the hall to their room, I braced myself so as not to appear shocked by the sick, dying person who awaited me. But as I entered, I found a smiling woman who seemed to be playing sick rather than someone genuinely near death's door.

Another honk sounded, and she threw a playful smile at her husband. "There goes the Harris family," she said. "It's good to hear from them again. I've missed them." He returned her smile.

After we were introduced, she explained that her life was now as rich as ever. Hundreds of times a day and throughout the night, she heard the chirps, trumpets, bleats, blasts, and roars of horns telling her that there is happiness in her world. "They have no idea I'm lying here listening," she said, "but I know them. I've gotten to where I know them by the sounds of their horns."

She blushed a little and then continued, "I've made up stories about them—I even give them names. I imagine the fun they're having at the beach or playing golf. If it's a rainy day, I imagine them going to the aquarium or shopping. At night I imagine them visiting the amusement park or dancing under the stars. They are leading happy lives. And that makes me happy. . . ." Her voice trailed off as she began to fall asleep. "Happy lives . . . what happy, happy lives."

Other than the honks outside the window, the three of us sat in silence for a few moments.

Finally, I looked at the coach. He smiled at me, and we both rose quietly and made our way out of the bedroom. He walked me to the door, but as I was about to leave a question came to me.

"You told me that the doctors had given her six months max to live, right?" I asked.

"That's right," he said with a smile that told me he knew my next question.

"But you said she was already sick and bedridden for several months before you put up the sign."

"Yep," he said.

"And I've driven by and seen the sign for well over a year now," I finished.

"Exactly," he said, patting me on the shoulder. And then he added, "Please come back and see us again, soon."

The HONK IF YOU'RE HAPPY sign was up for about another year, and then suddenly one day, it was gone.

"She must be dead," I thought sadly as I drove by. "At least she was happy in the end and beat the odds. Wouldn't her doctors be surprised."

A few days later I was driving along 544 toward the beach, and for the first time, I felt sadness rather

"What a wonderful life I've had! I only wish I'd realized it sooner."

—COLETTE

than happiness as I approached the causeway. I checked again, wondering if the wind or rain had simply ruined the fragile little sign. But it was indeed gone. I felt dark inside.

I kept thinking about this woman who, in the midst of pain, suffering, and death, had managed to find happiness in her world. I thought how so many people who have all that she would have wanted still walk around miserable and complaining.

The following week, I again found myself traveling along Highway 544 toward the beach. As I approached the causeway, my heart leapt as I saw something wonderful. Where the little cardboard-and-stick sign had once stood, there was now a new sign. It was a full six feet wide and four feet high with a bright yellow background bordered by dazzling, flashing lights. On both sides of the new sign, in large illuminated letters, was the familiar HONK IF YOU'RE HAPPY!

With tears in my eyes, I leaned on my horn to let the coach and his bride know I was passing. "There goes Will," I imagined her saying with a wistful smile.

With the support of her loving husband, rather than focusing on what her reality was, a reality confirmed by medical experts, this wonderful woman had focused on the happiness all around her. And, in so doing, she had beaten the odds, embraced life, and touched millions of people.

Life is not about where you stand, it's about the direction in which you are heading. And this is determined by where you are looking.

From the moment we first draw breath, we are moving toward the grave. When we'll get there, no one knows. The tragedy is not to die but to have never lived. To never have been happy where we are.

We tend to relegate happiness to "someday." When all of our problems are resolved, *then* we will be happy. The only time you will no longer have problems is the day when you exhale for the last time. Until then, there will be challenges and struggles, so you might as well make the decision—yes, the *decision*—to be happy.

Several years ago, I was in China to promote this book's being first published in Mandarin and I was having dinner with representatives from my Chinese publisher, Beijing Media Corporation. One of the dinner guests told me an ancient Chinese story about a woman who was always unhappy.

As the legend goes, the woman had two sons. One sold umbrellas to make a living and the other sold salt.

Every morning, the woman rose and looked out of her window. If she saw sunshine, she would complain, "Oh, this is terrible, no one will buy my son's umbrellas."

If she looked out of her window and saw rain, she would complain, "This is bad! No one will come and buy salt from my son."

After years of being despondent, she finally consulted a Buddhist monk, asking what she could do to find happiness.

His response was simple
and profound: "Change the
way you see things," he
said. "If it is raining, give
thanks that there will be

"Happiness is the only good. The
time to be happy is now; the place
to be happy is here."

—ROBERT G. INGERSOLL

demand for your son's umbrellas. If the sky is clear, celebrate
that people will come and buy salt from your other son."

She took his advice and her life quickly changed. The only
thing that changed was her perspective, but perspective is everything. Changing how we view the world causes us to see
new things and to see old things anew. Chronic complaining
keeps our focus on all things bad. Becoming Complaint Free
lets us see that there is much to be happy about.

The United States Declaration of Independence declares,
"We hold these truths to be self-evident, that all men are created equal, that they are endowed by their Creator with certain unalienable Rights, that among these are Life, Liberty and
the pursuit of Happiness."

Our modern understanding of the phrase "pursuit of Happiness" is not what Thomas Jefferson intended. In the late
1700s, the word *pursuit* had a very different meaning. Today,
the word *pursuit* means "going after something." Given this
perspective, we might believe that Jefferson meant we have
the right to "go after happiness."

However, to our colonial forefathers, the word *pursuit*
meant "something you practice," such as one might engage in
the pursuit (practice) of being a doctor, lawyer, businessper-
son, homemaker, or student. Someone in the 1700s might ask,

"What is your pursuit?" To which another would respond, "My pursuit is a blacksmith," or "a carpenter," or "a clothier."

To the founders of the United States, a pursuit was an activity in which one engaged, not the act of chasing after something. The Declaration of Independence therefore states that we have a God-given right to engage in happiness, not to chase after it.

The first step to practicing happiness is to claim that you *are* happy. You do this by ceasing to moan and gripe about your life and your experiences. Once you decide you are a happy person, you will naturally look for evidence to support your decision.

There is an admitted self-delusional quality to being happy. But there is also a self-delusional quality to being unhappy. Austrian philosopher Ludwig Wittgenstein said, "The world of those who are happy is different from the world of those who are not."

Life is an illusion. Our perspective is a delusion. Choose the delusion that brings you the only thing that matters—choose to be happy.

CHAPTER 9

COMMITMENT

*Until one is committed there is hesitancy, the chance to
draw back, always ineffectiveness. Concerning all acts of initiative
(and creation), there is one elementary truth, the ignorance of
which kills countless ideas and splendid plans: that the moment one
definitely commits oneself, then Providence moves too.*

—W. H. MURRAY

With every bump and turn of the earthmover, Korczak's leg hurt like hell.

After all these years, it seemed that pain was Korczak's constant, and often only, companion high up on Thunderhead Mountain.

Korczak Ziolkowski (pronounced "CORE-chalk Jewel-CUFF-ski"), a Polish immigrant to the United States, was a man on a mission. A mission born out of a commitment he had made decades before to create something the world had never seen, and he was not going to let a broken leg slow him down.

As he chugged along in the earthmover, pushing aside huge piles of dirt and rock, Korczak's pain was a relentless, bone-deep ache that caused him to grit his teeth. As he jos-

VOICES

I was there that weekend back in July of 2006 when Will handed out the very first Complaint Free bracelets and challenged us to go twenty-one days in a row without complaining.

I thought that it was a crazy idea! There's no way anyone could give up complaining. But I was shocked to see how many people around me embraced the idea so I gave it a try.

Trust me, this a very simple idea but to actually do it is very hard because it's so easy to quit!

My husband tried it with me at first but after just a few weeks he said it couldn't be done and he quit. He even began to tease me for being naïve enough to stay with it, but I did.

Every time I'd get a dozen or so days in, something would happen and I'd find myself complaining.

At one point, I remember wanting to throw that stupid bracelet out a window and give up but I didn't.

I kept at it. I wore that bracelet for so long and switched it so many times that the original purple began to wear off and it began to have a dirty gray color. But my bracelet became a badge of honor for me.

Then, finally, after more than a year and a half of trying, I made it! Twenty-one days without a single complaint and the best part is that I feel so much happier now.

I proved to myself (and my husband) that if I stayed with it, I could do it! I honestly believe anyone can do this if they just don't give up.

—HELEN MATTHEWS

KANSAS CITY, MISSOURI

tled about, the pain frequently became sharp, as if a knife were being stabbed into his thigh. In those moments, Korczak winced and cursed under his breath, but his progress never slowed.

This was not the first time Korczak had been injured while working to honor his commitment, and so far, nothing had slowed him down. Early in the project, he fell partway down the mountain and severely injured himself. A few years later, Korczak broke both his wrist and his thumb. Another time, while carrying his 80-pound jackhammer up the 741 rickety steps he'd built to the top of the mountain, Korczak slipped and fell, tearing his Achilles tendon.

After decades of schlepping his heavy tools up and down the mountain every day, Korczak had to have two major back surgeries that removed a total of three spinal discs. He had even suffered not one but two heart attacks, one of them severe, and yet he never stopped—ever. Each morning he was on the mountain around sunrise, and there he remained until long after sunset. Always working, never slowing, driven by his commitment.

"This busted leg was my own damn fault," Korczak muttered to himself as he maneuvered the earthmover around a huge boulder. "After all this time on the mountain, I should know to be more careful."

Just the day before, Korczak had miscalculated a turn and driven that very same earthmover off the side of the mountain. Both man and machine had careened, tumbled, and smashed their way down the side of Thunderhead Mountain before being abruptly stopped by a small cluster of trees. Had the trees not been there, Korczak would have probably died rather than just suffered a severely broken leg, which now pained him greatly.

"Take a few weeks off, maybe even a month, and let your leg heal," the doctor had said. Korczak smiled in response to the doctor's admonition, knowing that he would be back at his task the very next morning.

And he was.

Korczak had no official art training and yet here he was— creating the largest sculpture in human history. A sculpture he began in 1948 and one he knew he would never see completed during his lifetime.

Orphaned while only an infant, Korczak spent his youth living in foster homes. As a young teen, he was apprenticed to a shipbuilder as a woodcarver, and by the age of twenty, he had become an accomplished furniture maker.

But it was his job when he was thirty-one that made Korczak a dreamer of big dreams and helped him see what the human spirit was capable of creating. It was during that time Korczak served as an assistant to Gutzon Borglum during the creation of the Mount Rushmore memorial.

If you've ever seen Mount Rushmore, you know what an awe-inspiring spectacle it is. The problem is that Mount Rushmore is situated in sacred hills that for millennia had been home to several Native American tribes. There, in the middle of their hallowed lands, the United States had placed a monument to past presidents. Presidents who represented to the tribespeople more than a hundred years of broken treaties, abuse, and death.

"Commitment is what transforms a promise into a reality."

—ABRAHAM LINCOLN

The unveiling of Mount Rushmore inspired more than a dozen Indian chiefs to commit to the creation of a monument to celebrate their people and their lands.

Henry Standing Bear, chief of the Ponca tribe, said in a famous speech to his brethren, "My fellow chiefs and I would like the white man to know the red man has great heroes, too."

Henry Standing Bear was designated the leader of this project and he set about trying to find an artist who not only was up to the task but would work for free—yes, free—to construct the enormous statue.

Several artists were considered, but it was Korczak Ziolkowski's passion that convinced Henry Standing Bear and his fellow chiefs that he was the right man for the job. Korczak envisioned something even bigger than the largest sculpture in human history. He wanted to surround the monument with a Native American cultural center and even a free university exclusively for American Indians.

As to the monument, Korczak's idea was that it had to dwarf Mount Rushmore not only in size but also in artistic scope. Mount Rushmore shows only the top half and front side of presidents Washington, Jefferson, Lincoln, and Roosevelt, whereas Korczak's vision was a 360-degree sculpture showing all sides of the famous person being represented.

When it came to selecting the Native American to be immortalized in granite, the choice was obvious—the great Heyoka and chief mentioned in chapter 3, Crazy Horse.

A member of the Oglala Lakota tribe, he was named Cha-O-Ha at birth, although his mother called him "Light Hair." Cha-O-Ha distinguished himself in battle many times as a young brave, and as a result, he was awarded the high honor of being able to take his father's name as his own. Cha-O-Ha's father was named Tasunke Witco, which translates to "His Horses Are Crazy." White settlers later shortened that to "Crazy Horse."

Before beginning the project, Korczak invested seven years reading, studying, and learning all he could about Native American culture and history. Then, in 1948, at the age of forty, he moved with his wife, Ruth, to the Badlands of South Dakota and began. The rest of his life's work stood there waiting to be revealed as he drilled, dynamited, and sculpted Thunderhead Mountain.

Korczak and Chief Henry Standing Bear had selected Thunderhead Mountain, and it's only a coincidence that young Crazy Horse had dreamed of thunder, leading him to become a Heyoka, or "thunder dreamer."

The planned monument is of a shirtless Crazy Horse from the waist up atop his horse Inyan, his hair and the horse's mane billowing in the breeze as the great chief points to his ancestral lands. The significance of this gesture is that Crazy Horse was once derisively asked by a U.S. cavalryman, "Where are your lands now?" to which Crazy Horse responded, "My lands are where my dead lie buried."

When the Crazy Horse Memorial is finished it will be 563 feet high and 641 feet wide. It will be so big

"Commitment is an act, not a word."

—JEAN-PAUL SARTRE

that all of Mount Rushmore will fit easily in the space occupied by just Crazy Horse's head.

And true to his word, Korczak never received a penny for his work. He sold paintings and sculptures he created in the evening after long days on the mountain so that all money received by the Crazy Horse Memorial Foundation could be used exclusively for supplies and equipment to fulfill his commitment.

Twice, the United States government offered Korczak ten million dollars to move the project along to completion, and both times he refused. Korczak believed it would be a breach of his integrity to accept money from the very government that had driven the Indians off their lands.

For thirty-four years, during the sweltering heat of South Dakota summers and the biting cold of its winters, Korczak worked every day—no vacation, no holidays, and definitely no sick days.

While the rest of the world celebrated Christmas, he was on the mountain working to honor his commitment. And yet, when he died at age seventy-four not a single discernible characteristic of Crazy Horse was visible. He died in 1982, and it was not until 1998—a full sixteen years later—that the face, just the face, of Crazy Horse, was completed. If the face were laid on its side it would be the length of three football fields. It bears a striking resemblance to historic descriptions of the great chief, and to date, more than seventy-five years after Korczak Ziolkowski's work began, the face and part of a rough-hewn arm are all that have been completed.

As you read this, seven of Korczak's ten children are on the mountain continuing the work their father started, knowing that they, too, are unlikely to see their father's vision completed.

Such is the nature of commitment. Commitment doesn't make excuses. It never blames outside circumstances. And it never takes a day off. I've never known anyone who failed at the twenty-one-day Complaint Free challenge, but there are lots of people who have simply lost their commitment and given up.

Several times as I've concluded a speech and gone out to the lobby to sign autographs and take selfies with attendees, people have said to me some variation of "You know, I think that the Complaint Free challenge is a great idea and I can really see the benefit. But my life is really difficult right now, so when things get better for me, I'm going to give it a try." When I hear this, I think to myself, "Yes, and as soon as I get in great shape, I'm going to start going to the gym."

The time to take the Complaint Free challenge is when your life *is* a struggle, because ceasing to complain will shift your focus to possibilities rather than limitations. As a result, your life will begin to improve. But it's not enough to just take the challenge, you have to stay with it!

President Calvin Coolidge famously said this about the power of commitment:

Nothing in this world can take the place of persistence. Talent will not; nothing is more common than unsuccessful men with talent. Genius will not; unrewarded genius is almost a proverb. Education will not; the world is full of educated derelicts. Persistence and determination alone are omnipotent. The slogan "Press On!" has solved and always will solve the problems of the human race.

For you to enjoy all the benefits of Complaint Free living, including increased happiness, improved health, and better relationships, you must press on even when life is tough.

If you're like most people, when you begin this process, you will probably move your bracelet from arm to arm until you get sore and tired of doing it. But if you just stay with it, one day you'll be lying in bed about to drift off to sleep, and you'll glance at your wrist. There, for the first time in days or possibly weeks, you'll see that your purple bracelet is on the same wrist as when you got out of bed that morning. You'll think, "I must have complained at some point today and just not caught myself." But as you do a mental inventory, you'll

"When your life is over, the world will ask you only one question: 'Did you do what you were supposed to do?'"

—KORCZAK ZIOLKOWSKI

realize that you made it. You actually made it one whole day without complaining! One day at a time. You can do it.

Without a doubt, the single greatest personal development book of all time is *Think and Grow Rich* by Napoleon Hill. Originally published in 1937, this single work has set more people on the path to wealth and happiness than any other.

Just this past year, I read another book by Napoleon Hill titled *Outwitting the Devil,* which was published a full forty-one years after Hill's death. The story is an allegory in which the author interviews Satan himself and demands to know how the Prince of Darkness manages to thwart the health and happiness of so many people.

"It all comes down to drifting," the Devil states. Drifting is when you know what you want and maybe even make plans to attain it, but your focus drifts here and there to other things and you lose focus on what really matters. Drifting kills all great plans because it scatters your attention away from what's really important.

To keep your commitment to the Complaint Free challenge, you cannot afford to drift. You must wear your purple bracelet every day and be diligent with switching it to the other wrist, starting over on Day 1, with every complaint.

The only way for you to fail at the Complaint Free challenge is by letting yourself drift to other seeming priorities such that you lose your commitment. Don't allow this to happen. More than one hundred years ago, the poet Edgar A. Guest gave us the secret to success when his poem "Keep Going" was published in newspapers around the United States:

Keep Going

When things go wrong, as they sometimes will,
When the road you're trudging seems all up hill,
When the funds are low and the debts are high,
And you want to smile, but you have to sigh,
When care is pressing you down a bit,
Rest if you must—but don't you quit.

Life is queer with its twists and turns,
As every one of us sometimes learns,
And many a failure turns about
When he might have won had he stuck it out;
Don't give up, though the pace seems slow—
You may succeed with another blow.

Often the goal is nearer than
It seems to a faint and faltering man,
Often the struggler has given up
When he might have captured the victor's cup,
And he learned too late, when the night slipped down,
How close he was to the golden crown.

Success is failure turned inside out—
The silver tint of the clouds of doubt,
And you never can tell how close you are,
It may be near when it seems afar;
So stick to the fight when you're hardest hit—
It's when things seem worst that you mustn't quit.

PART 4

UNCONSCIOUS COMPETENCE

CHAPTER 10

MASTERY

The sun was shining in my eyes, and I could barely see;
To do the necessary task that was allotted me.
Resentment of the vivid glow I started to complain.
When all at once upon the air I heard the blind man's cane.

—EARL MUSSELMAN

There are several species of fish known as blind cave fish. Some of them can be found in the United States, in the limestone cave regions of the Mississippi Delta. Blind cave fish grow up to five inches in length and have little or no pigmentation. In addition to their pale skin, all but one of the species has no eyes. Scientists conjecture that many years ago these fish's ancestors may have been trapped by shifts in the landmass or water channels and become cave-bound. Surrounded entirely by darkness and unable to see, the fish adapted to their surroundings. These species of fish now thrive in total darkness.

Over generations of having offspring, blind cave fish ceased to produce pigmentation to protect their skin from the sun because it was no longer necessary. Similarly, over time, blind cave fish began to give birth to fry without eyes.

After you have undergone the months it takes to become a

Complaint Free person, you will find that you've changed. Just as over generations the bodies of blind cave fish stopped producing both pigmentation and eyes, you'll find that your mind no longer produces a deluge of negativity. Because you are not articulating negative thoughts, the complaint factory in your mind closes down. You have shut off the spigot and the well has dried up. By changing your words, you have reshaped the way you think. It has now become unconscious (you don't notice) for you to be competent (not complain).

I conducted a seminar on becoming Complaint Free and wanted the audience to see how heavy and negative the energy in the room felt when everyone complained. I also wanted them to get some practice switching their bracelets with each complaint, so I invited everyone to pair off and take turns complaining and switching their bracelets.

I noticed that one woman did not have anyone to be her partner, so I offered to do the assignment with her. She went first, complaining about her mother. After she switched her bracelet, she looked at me expectantly, indicating that it was my turn to complain. I stood in silence. I could not think of anything to complain about, and even when I did conjure something up, I realized it was very hard to form the words.

After many months of constantly watching every word I said, my mind had changed. The factory had shut down the complaint department. Further, I had become so focused on catching and pre-

"Before you complain today be grateful you have breath to complain with."

—LECRAE

VOICES

Four years ago my twenty-three-yr.-old son (my oldest), a police officer, suffered a bleed in his brain while driving. Without going into details, it has been a long road, but one that my whole family has faced with trust in God and unconditional love.

Ben is recovering (all the docs said he wouldn't make it) and he accepts his disabilities with a peace that is such a lesson for us all. God's grace is active and growing in him.

He has mild aphasia, right side weakness, and some slower processing yet he continues to improve—all without complaining. Thus, the reason for the bracelets. If Ben can accept his cross without complaining surely the rest of us can. I want people who have helped Ben in his recovery to all get a bracelet.

Thank you so much and continued GOOD LUCK with your mission. You have made an impact!

—NOREEN KEPPLE
STONINGTON, CONNECT

venting myself from complaining, I felt as if lightning might strike me if I did complain.

I was now Unconsciously Competent. I had become to complaining what blind cave fish have become to light. I had lost the capacity and the ability to complain. And what was most important was that I found I was much happier for having made the effort to change.

This is why we give a "Certificate of Happiness" rather than a "Complaint Free Certificate" whenever someone completes the twenty-one-day challenge. Because the experience of becoming happier has been so universal for those who have stayed with the challenge, we want to acknowledge the real transformation that takes place.

When you successfully complete your twenty-one days, send us an email at CustomerService@WillBowen.com and we'll create a Certificate of Happiness for you to download. It is a real accomplishment to have stayed with this, and your life will reflect your efforts in positive and exciting ways.

In the Unconscious Competence stage, you are no longer an "ouch" looking for a hurt. Rather, your thoughts are now on what you want, and you are beginning to notice how what you desire manifests. Not only are you happier, but also the people around you seem happier. You are attracting upbeat people, and your positive nature is inspiring those around you to even higher mental and emotional levels. To paraphrase Gandhi, you have become the change you wish to see in your world. When a challenge presents itself, you don't give it any energy by complaining about it to others; rather, you speak directly and only to those who can resolve your issue.

During this stage, you'll notice how uncomfortable you now feel when someone around you begins to complain. It's as if a very unpleasant odor has suddenly wafted into the room. Because you've spent so much time checking yourself against complaining, when you hear complaints coming from someone else it's like a clanging cymbal during a moment of sacred silence. Even though the person's griping isn't pleasant for you to hear, you won't feel compelled to correct them. Rather, you'll sim-

> "Champions never complain, they are too busy getting better."
>
> —JOHN WOODEN

ply observe the complaining, and because you neither criticize nor complain, the person won't need to justify and perpetuate their behavior.

You will begin to feel gratitude for the smallest things. Even things you used to take for granted. As you settle into being Unconsciously Competent, your default mindset will be one of appreciation. You will still have things you desire to obtain, and that's good. Now, with your newfound positive energy, you can hold an image in your mind of what you desire, knowing that it is moving toward you.

Your financial situation will probably improve as well. Money is, in and of itself, without value. Money is slips of paper and coins that *represent* value. As you begin to value yourself and your world more, you will vibrate at a level that attracts greater financial benefits.

Watch for the smallest acts of kindness or generosity and be grateful. If someone holds a door open for you or offers to carry something for you, count it as an abundant blessing from the Universe, and in so doing, you'll attract more.

You'll become a ray of sunshine in the lives of others rather than a cloud of doom, and life will reward you for your new way of being.

I used to work for a radio station in Seattle, Washington.

Our receptionist was named Martha. Martha had the widest, brightest, and most sincere smile I've ever seen. She was always complimentary, genuinely happy, and willing to do anything for anyone. You could feel her presence in the office, and everyone was more cheerful and productive when Martha was around.

A few years after I stopped working there, I went back by the station to visit some friends. Something was different. As I stood in the lobby, the whole energy and ambiance seemed to have changed. It was as if someone had painted the walls a darker color or perhaps the lighting had gone bad.

"Where's Martha?" I asked.

The sales manager sighed. "She was hired away for more than twice what we were paying her." She gazed slowly around the office and then added with a frown, "That company got a deal!"

Martha's happy, upbeat personality radiated out to everyone at the station, and her leaving had brought the overall level of happiness and productivity down. Salespeople said that client complaints increased in both number and vehemence without Martha there to sprinkle her sweetness onto customers when they called in.

One of the greatest gifts of becoming a Complaint Free person is the impact you will have on your family. Your children will begin not only to model your behavior but to adopt your outlook on life. They will be entrained by you and begin to see things as you see them.

As a parent, grandparent, aunt, or uncle, you are modeling how impressionable youngsters will behave. Children become like the adults they see. Now that you know how destructive complaining is, do you really want your children to grow up to become habitual complainers? Do you want them to adopt a gloomy worldview and to feel like disempowered victims? Of course not.

> "People won't have time for you if you are always angry or complaining."
>
> **—STEPHEN HAWKING**

After a recent speech, a woman approached me and stridently asked, "How do I get my ungrateful kids to stop griping about every little thing?" She then proceeded to complain to me in great detail about all the problems she had with her children.

"Perhaps you might work at becoming Complaint Free yourself," I told the haggard mom, knowing that her children were just mirroring back her words and attitude.

She shot me an exasperated glance and said, "I wouldn't complain if it wasn't for my darn kids!"

Sigh.

This mom was caught in a loop of negativity and didn't want to accept that I had just pointed out an off-ramp to her. Worse, she was setting her kids up for an unhappy and unfulfilling life.

A person who doesn't complain tends to get what they want more easily simply because other people want to help an agreeable person more than they want to help someone who berates and harangues them. Now that you have become Complaint Free, people are going to want to work with and for you, and you will achieve and receive more than you ever dreamed. Give it time. Watch for it. It will happen.

I'm often asked, "But what about social causes that I'm passionate about? How can I help bring about positive change if I don't complain?" As we've discussed, all change begins with dissatisfaction. It begins when someone sees a gap between what is and what could be. Dissatisfaction is the beginning but it cannot be the end.

If you complain about a situation, you may be able to draw others to you, but you won't be able to get much done because your focus is on the problem and not the solution. Figure out what needs to be done and then begin to speak in terms of what it will be like when the challenge no longer exists, when the gap is bridged, when the problem is solved. You will then excite people to join you in improving things.

Another benefit of not complaining is that you will find yourself angry and afraid less often. Anger is fear directed outward. And because you are no longer a fearful person, you will attract fewer angry and fearful people into your life.

I have a friend who was the minister of a church in a small town. The sanctioning body for his religion sent a consultant to help him grow his congregation.

"Find something your flock is afraid of," the consultant said. "Use that to get them angry. They'll complain about the situation to others; this will unify them and draw more people into your church."

This approach seemed to lack integrity to my friend, who saw the purpose of his ministry as serving those in need and filling them with hope rather than riling up an angry mob. Calling one of his fellow ministers, he asked how this fearmongering approach had worked for his church.

"Well, you could say that it worked well," the other minister said. "It brought in a lot of new people. The problem is that they're a bunch of angry and fearful people who complain all the time—and now I'm stuck dealing with them."

If you want to see a great example of complaining used to build a following, watch the classic movie *The Music Man* starring Robert Preston. Preston plays the fast-talking and unscrupulous salesman Professor Harold Hill, who peddles band instruments. Arriving in River City, Iowa, Professor Hill asks an old friend, played by Buddy Hackett, "What is something happening here in River City that I can use to get the citizens upset?" Hackett tells him that the latest big news is that the town's first pool table has just arrived.

Professor Hill seizes on this event, singing a song that stirs up the fears of the townspeople about the delinquency and degeneracy that he says are a natural extension of young people playing pool.

> "When life gives you lemons, make lemonade and sell it to all of those who get thirsty from complaining."
>
> **—NAPOLEON HILL**

Hill's solution to the "moral corruption" and "mass hysteria" pool playing brings is for all the young men in town to join a band. And Professor Harold Hill, salesman extraordinaire, is there to save the day by selling all the boys' parents band instruments and uniforms. He complains to manipulate the townsfolk for his own profit, and it works.

I'm often asked, "But isn't complaining healthy? Don't you need to vent your frustrations to get rid of them?"

The idea of venting negative emotions became popular in the United States during the 1970s when some psychologists encouraged patients to engage in what was called "scream therapy." The belief was that a person could exhaust the negativity and pain they held inside by screaming it away. This approach has since been debunked.

Dr. Brad Bushman, research professor at the Institute for Social Research at the Ohio State University, has spent nearly thirty-five years researching anger. He states, "Our research clearly shows that venting angry feelings *increases* aggressive inclinations, it does not decrease them."

In an article posted on the website the Inquisitive Mind, Bushman writes about catharsis theory—the psychological term for the idea that venting anger will reduce it:

Catharsis theory holds that expressing anger produces a healthy release of emotion and is therefore good for the psyche. Catharsis theory, which can be traced back through Sigmund Freud to Aristotle, is elegant and appealing. Unfortunately, the facts and findings do not

show that venting one's anger has positive value. It
harms the self and others.

Penn and Teller, the Las Vegas magicians and famous debunkers of popular myths, engaged Dr. Bushman to prove this point on their Showtime network program *Bulls**t!*

Bushman invited six college students to take part in a psychological experiment. Each student was placed in a small room, given a pen and a piece of paper, and asked to write an essay on any topic of their choosing. After approximately thirty minutes, Bushman's research assistant John collected the papers and told each of them to wait while another student graded their papers.

In reality, there was no other student to grade the papers. John took a red marker and wrote, "F! Worst essay I've ever read!" in big letters at the top of each paper. He then returned the "graded" essays to the students. In the video, you can see the anger on the students' faces for having received such a critical review of their work.

John then brought in a pillow to three of the six students and asked them to punch the pillow for several minutes to release the anger caused by the incident.

The other three students, the control group, were given time to simply sit quietly and feel their anger.

John waited awhile and then returned to each of the students and

"If you stop complaining and asking for what you never will get, you will have a good life."

—ERNEST HEMINGWAY

told them they now had a chance to exact revenge on the "student who had so harshly graded their paper." Remember, there *was* no other student; John had written the failing grade and the critical comment on each of the essays to make the students angry.

Entering the room in which each student sat, John carried a tray containing fiery hot sauce and a cup. He informed the students that they could choose how much hot sauce the fictitious "other student" would have to drink. After the students poured as much of the blistering liquid into the cups as they felt was appropriate, the cups were then weighed.

Here's the interesting part: The students who had hit the pillow, and thereby vented their anger, poured *much* more hot sauce into their cups.

Take that in for a moment. The popular catharsis or anger-venting theory would have us believe that the students who pounded a pillow should have released their anger, but in reality, after having been allowed to vent to their hearts' content, the students who punched a pillow held *more* anger and *more* resentment than the ones given a chance to just sit quietly for a few moments.

Bushman states, "The results of our study show that people who vent their anger are about twice as aggressive as those who do nothing at all."

There was a second part to this study that even more dramatically demonstrates how venting *increases* rather than diminishes upset. Each of the students in the experiment was given a sheet of paper containing a list of partial words and was asked to fill in missing letters for each. The list included:

C h o _ e
A t t _ c _
K i _ _
R _ p _

The students in the control group who had *not* been given the opportunity to punch the pillow to vent their anger tended to fill in the missing letters creating neutral words, such as:

C h o s e
A t t a c h
K i t e
R o p e

However, the students who had vented by punching the pillow, who, according to conventional wisdom, should have expelled their anger and become more centered and peaceful, tended to complete the words as:

C h o k e
A t t a c k
K i l l
R a p e

"When angry, count ten before you speak; if very angry, a hundred."
—THOMAS JEFFERSON

"Aggression becomes *more* likely after venting," Bushman explains. In short, this whole idea of venting anger away is a myth that has been accepted and popularized by counselors, psychologists, and the media for decades, but it actually accomplishes the exact opposite.

In a paper titled "Catharsis, Aggression, and Persuasive Influence: Self-Fulfilling or Self-Defeating Prophecies?," which Dr. Bushman coauthored with Roy F. Baumeister and Angela D. Stack, the researchers state, "Participants who read a pro-catharsis message claiming that aggressive action is a good way to relax and reduce anger subsequently expressed a greater desire to hit a punching bag."

And, after decades of similar studies of cathartic anger, psychology professor Jeffrey Lohr of the University of Arkansas found the same result. His research concludes, "Punching pillows and breaking dishes doesn't reduce subsequent anger expression. That, the research shows clearly. In fact, the research very clearly shows the opposite is true: The more you get angry, the angrier you get."

Common experience proves that venting does not make us feel better. If venting anger made people happier, then wouldn't the biggest complainers you know also be the happiest people? We all know that's not true. As Bushman writes, "People who have problems dealing with their anger, if they go to see a therapist who has them vent their anger, they need to find a new therapist, fast!"

Michael Cunningham, PhD, a psychologist at Tulane University, explains that the human predilection for complaining probably evolved from our ancestors' way of crying out a warning when something threatened the tribe. "We mammals are a squealing species," Cunningham says. "We talk about things that bother us as a way of getting help or seeking a posse to mount a counterattack."

When we complain, we are saying, "Something is wrong." When we complain often, we live in a perpetual state of "something is wrong," and this increases stress in our lives.

Imagine if someone were constantly shadowing you saying things such as "Beware!" or "Watch out—something bad is going to happen!" or "Something bad that happened in the past means more bad things are coming." Wouldn't it make your life more stressful if someone were repeatedly pointing out possible dangers and pitfalls?

Of course it would. And when you complain frequently, the person sounding the warning alarm is you! You are raising your stress level by complaining. You are saying, "Something is wrong," and your body responds with high levels of stress.

In "Complaints and Complaining: Functions, Antecedents, and Consequences," Dr. Robin Kowalski sums up the impact of complaining on our bodies succinctly, stating, "Symptoms increase with symptom reporting." In other words, the more you complain about your life and your health, the more problems you'll experience.

I'm frequently asked, "Is it okay to talk about my problems with my therapist, or is that complaining?" And the answer is yes, of course you can, because when you're talking to a therapist you're speaking directly and only to someone who can help resolve your issue. A good therapist can give painful experiences in your life meaning and provide hope and constructive paradigms for better living.

However, venting to a friend, co-worker, family member, or stranger who can only commiserate with you will be an excuse for unbridled negativity that will actually draw more problems to you. And exposing yourself to other negative, complaining people fires off negative regions of your brain, making you more likely to focus on what's wrong and miss rather than be grateful for what's present and working.

An article in *Inc.* magazine explains this phenomenon: "When we see someone experiencing an emotion (be it anger, sadness, happiness, etc.), our brain 'tries out' that same emotion to imagine what the other person is going through. And it does this by attempting to fire the same synapses in your own brain so that you can attempt to relate to the emotion you're observing." Therefore, as we've discussed previously, excusing yourself when people begin to complain or express negativity is actually good for both your physical and your mental health.

Remember that the opposite of complaining is gratitude. Invest time writing out a daily gratitude list. Give thanks for what's good in your life and you won't have time to focus on what's wrong. Research conducted at the University of California, Davis, found that people who worked daily to cultivate an attitude of gratitude reduced the stress hormone cortisol a whopping 23 percent and, as a result, enjoyed better moods and more energy.

There is an old saying: "When you're in a hole, stop digging." If your life up to this point has not been the way you want it to be, then stop digging the hole deeper by complaining. Complete the twenty-one-day Complaint Free challenge by staying with it. Every aspect of your life will improve.

In the next chapter, you'll hear from people who have seen the power of the Complaint Free challenge in their own lives.

CHAPTER 11

COMPLAINT FREE STORIES

Those who do not complain are never pitied.
—JANE AUSTEN

This chapter is dedicated to just some of the more than fifteen million people who have taken the Complaint Free challenge thus far.

As you read their stories, notice common themes and also see if you can find aspects of yourself in their experiences.

WAZHMA MASARWEH
Preschool Director

I had the opportunity to attend the 2022 Association for Early Childhood Educators conference in Dallas, Texas, where Will was one of the keynote speakers.

Immediately, I became focused on everything he was saying, including the purple bracelets and the Complaint Free challenge. I texted my assistant director, showing her pictures of Will's PowerPoint slides, and said, "Erika, we are going to do this!"

That night in the hotel I downloaded Will's book *A Complaint Free World* from Audible and I opened up Will's Facebook page to become part of the Complaint Free group. I had a new mission and couldn't wait to share it with my family and co-workers.

When I arrived back home, I told my husband and my daughters all about the Complaint Free challenge. I next held an all-staff meeting with my teachers and I told them there would be a big incentive for anyone who would join me in the Complaint Free challenge. I saw an excited show of hands! The next day I ordered the bracelets and kept listening to Will's audiobook for more inspiration and help on this journey.

I became aware of how I used words and how they sounded. I found myself complaining less about traffic or getting upset about messes left by others at our house. The times that I did get off track were mainly at work, where I had to keep reminding myself that I must set an example for those joining me on the challenge by not complaining about parents, other teachers, etc. So, I kept changing my bracelet from wrist to wrist.

The first three weeks were hard. Nevertheless, I kept at it and pretty soon the challenge became a no-brainer. I officially completed my Complaint Free challenge on June 5th, 2022. I not only finished reading the book *A Complaint Free World* but I still periodically reread portions of it. I have also read Will's book *Complaint Free Relationships* several times both in hard copy and audio versions.

Since taking the twenty-one-day Complaint Free challenge, I have completely stopped exposing myself to news, choosing instead what makes me happy vs. what makes me sad.

I have learned we only get one life, and we have to live it to the fullest. My relationships with my husband, my daughters, and myself all have new meaning now! I am a continuing work in progress, and I appreciate my new outlook on life.

WENDY BABCOCK

Speaker, Founder of the Kindness Bucket Brigade

The Complaint Free challenge changed my life in every way possible. Yes, I know that sounds dramatic, but it's absolutely true. When I stumbled across this movement, I was working a full-time job at a local hospital and was getting to the point of really disliking my job.

In the twenty years I had worked there, I had never experienced that feeling of dread walking through the door each morning like I was now experiencing. I had recently switched positions from the lead medical transcriptionist to a medical coder. It was a difficult change, and it was not a good fit for me. Besides my unhappiness at work, I was also still working on myself; having left an abusive marriage ten years prior, I was still struggling with PTSD and working on becoming a better person.

I was listening to an Audible book by Pam Grout when she mentioned the Complaint Free movement. I recall pausing the audiobook to ponder that. A Complaint Free world? I thought about all the ways in which I was trying to push negativity out of my life to create a better future for myself. Stopping complaining, I thought, was the best thing I could do. If I was to eliminate complaining from my life, I wondered what kind of effects it would make. I quickly went to Google and social media to search for this movement and its creator, Will Bowen. I read about the impact this movement already had on millions of people and I was intrigued!

On social media I found Will Bowen's business profile to learn more about who he is. I would call this next moment in time fate because, that very day, Will Bowen posted that he was looking for ten people he could train to speak about *A Complaint Free World* to make an even larger impact on the world.

Before I could even really think about it, I was sending off an email to apply, but as soon as I clicked the "send" button, I had a panic attack. Reality hit me like a ton of bricks! "I'm not a speaker," I said to myself. "I hate talking in front of an audience full of people!" I sat there asking myself why on earth I had applied to train to become a motivational speaker and fretted until I realized there was a very good chance I would not be chosen.

However, about two weeks later, I received an email from someone on Will Bowen's team stating, "We are so excited about your interest in becoming a Complaint Free Certified Trainer! I would like to set up an interview with you."

When it was time for my Skype interview, I was so nervous, but I was met with a very welcoming smile from the young lady on the other side of the screen. She was reassuring, bubbly, and made me feel right at home talking to her. That's when I learned that this was Will Bowen's daughter, Amelia.

She asked me questions about why I felt I would be a good fit for this training. I suddenly realized I was giving her my life story, detailing how I had overcome so much. From a painful childhood and domestic abuse to having just undergone a bilateral mastectomy, I shared with her all the techniques I used to keep my mindset positive and to heal my life.

After the interview I waited for what seemed like an eternity and then one day I heard a "ding!" alerting me to an incoming email. I then read the words that would change my life forever, "Congratulations, you've been selected!"

I was shocked, excited, panicked, elated . . . and so many other emotions all at once. I resolved that because they put their faith in me, I would give this my all. I would show up, do the training, and put my best foot forward. And I did just that. That summer, my husband and I drove from central Wisconsin to Kansas City, Missouri, where I was officially certified by Will Bowen as a Complaint Free Trainer.

Thanks to Will's training, I started to book speaking engagements. I spoke at some churches, a local school, and several community groups. I felt exhilarated after each presentation! I began feeling more and more comfortable being onstage.

That August, my dad lost his battle with his third bout of cancer. Understandably, our family was devastated. It was during a moment in my grief when I realized life is too short to do anything other than what makes me happy. I had a heart-to-heart talk with my husband about quitting my job and pursuing a speaking career full-time. He was so supportive and wanted to see me happy and successful, and so I hit the ground running and booked as many speaking engagements as I could.

Soon, I was booking speaking engagements out of state and got to travel to some really cool places. My husband Brian traveled with me and we created some mini vacations around these bookings. Thanks to the virtual opportunities created during the COVID pandemic, I was then able to start speaking internationally to people in Australia and the United Kingdom. Then, in August 2021, I presented at my first TEDx event!

So, when I say the Complaint Free challenge changed my life in every way, I mean it! Not only did it change my mindset, my relationships, and my lifestyle, it changed the way I look at life. Instead of complaining about what life has thrown my way, I now ask myself, "What's going well in my life?" and I always find an answer!

KENNY HERBOLD

Actuarial and Financial Professional

I have never really considered myself a complainer, but I believe in continual self-improvement so when I heard a woman mention Will and the Complaint Free challenge on her podcast, I knew it was something I had to check out.

Especially when the podcast presenter mentioned that she was working on making sure that whenever she had a problem, she spoke directly and only to the person who could fix it, rather than complain.

The Complaint Free challenge took me down a fantastic road of self-discovery. Taking the challenge was an intense crash course in self-awareness that I'm not sure you will find anywhere else. I'm not claiming that I have become some fully enlightened guru, but the focus necessary to really hear your thoughts and ultimately learn to correct those thoughts before speaking them aloud requires a high level of awareness that can be extremely hard to develop.

The Complaint Free challenge pushes you to that level of self-mastery. I was able to develop the habit of removing certain types of speech and topics from my vocabulary. For example, I worked hard to eliminate gossip from my conversations as well as complaining patterns that used to plague me.

Now, don't get me wrong, I still had occasional days when I came home and just had to tell my wife about what so-and-so did or what that idiot co-worker had done to ruin my day, but those incidents became few and far between.

What I really started noticing was how certain behaviors from other people impacted my mood. I found that my wife complaining about something, especially if it was something I thought was "dumb," would put me in a bad mood. That negativity would send our evenings into a tailspin because when I reacted poorly to what she was complaining about, she would then react negatively toward me, and we would become frustrated with one another for no good reason.

I even became aware of how if I disliked how someone else was driving I would verbalize my complaints in the car, as if that would make them drive better.

It took me almost eight months to string together twenty-one consecutive days without a single complaint. On that journey, I became a much more patient driver. But most importantly, I learned how to recognize when other people's emotions and actions, things over which I have no control and that don't really impact my life much at all, had a negative impact on my mood. That alone has allowed me to accept the things I cannot change and has brought a calmer, more positive approach to my relationships and life in general.

ANDY HAUSMANN

Client Success Manager

I enjoy reading anything that will improve my life and one day I came across *A Complaint Free World* by Will Bowen. I was really inspired by the positive message so after I read the book, I decided to take the twenty-one-day Complaint Free challenge.

Within a few days of starting the challenge, I started feeling lighter and happier and, most importantly, my marriage with my wife Gina improved as we began to communicate in a more loving and effective manner. Plus, I found I had better energy when I got home from work. I even became a more positive father to my son Brody and daughter Bella. I no longer complain or get upset if they throw a tantrum.

One of the things I appreciate the most about taking the twenty-one-day challenge is how I'm attracting more positivity into my life. I've become more intentional about what I say and how I say it. And I now find myself responding instead of reacting.

I also notice that when other people complain, criticize, or gossip I make a conscious effort not to get caught up in it. After a while, I even stopped joining in on any type of negativity at work. My best streak of no complaining so far has been thirteen days, and I am looking forward to successfully completing Day 21.

Taking the twenty-one-day challenge has made a very positive impact on my life, and I'm so grateful for that. Although it is not easy, I enjoy the process and will be taking the challenge on a regular basis from now on.

KATHI CRUZ

Construction Estimator

When the 2020 pandemic hit, I found myself with a lot more time to be introspective and also looking for things to do at home. I had heard of *A Complaint Free World* but had not read the book yet. I started searching the internet and found Will Bowen's daily "JumpStarts" on his Facebook page.

I began watching the JumpStarts daily. That led me to join Will's Complaint Free Life Inner Circle, buy his book, and get a purple bracelet. I am still a work in progress to make it to twenty-one days, but this group keeps me focused and aware of my thoughts and actions. I know I'll make it to twenty-one days!

I love the feeling of belonging, accountability, and support in the Complaint Free Life Inner Circle. The group gives me positive encouragement with daily posts and cheering one another on as we progress or start back on Day 1. It is an inspiring group and I'm very happy I joined.

Twenty-one days Complaint Free here I come!

LIZ DOUCETTE SNEDDON

Entrepreneur

In November 2020, I first heard about A Complaint Free World when I heard Will being interviewed on this brilliant concept. I was intrigued. It definitely caught my attention.

Several weeks went by and my mind would still wander back to that interview. So, I decided to put myself through a test.

How many days could I go without complaining?

I quickly realized that it would be best to start by seeing how many of my waking hours I could go without complaining.

I've always thought of myself as a positive person but becoming aware of my words was startling to me. I realized I had a lot of work to do so I ordered Will's book *A Complaint Free World* and absorbed its concepts. I ordered a Complaint Free bracelet for myself as well as a few extras in hopes of having other people join me in the twenty-one-day Complaint Free challenge. Next, I joined the Complaint Free Life Inner Circle, which I have also found to be a powerful tool. By tracking and reporting daily where I am in my twenty-one-day journey, it helps to keep my awareness alive.

The experience has been one of incredible personal growth. This concept, the book, and the social support I receive from the Complaint Free Life Inner Circle have definitely been power tools in my growth. It took me 230 days to complete the 21-day Complaint Free challenge, but I made it!

My focus is now on gratitude, the strengths in people around me, the kindness in others, and searching for the lesson within each challenge. My goal now is to make at least one person smile each day! Thank you, Will Bowen! I am grateful for you and I appreciate you!

LINDA STARNES

Retired Teacher, Founder of Just Say Whoa

More than a decade ago, I first took the Complaint Free challenge after reading Will Bowen's book *A Complaint Free World* and it inspired me to not only stop complaining but to start a program for kids and horses.

Will Bowen came back into my world when I discovered his daily JumpStart videos and I ordered his book again, took the Complaint Free challenge, and joined the Complaint Free Life Inner Circle.

Will Bowen has made a positive difference in the world and in my life.

The twenty-one-day Complaint Free challenge changes your mind to thinking positively and being grateful, which inspires you to help other people.

I am now in a different place thanks to this program. I am a grateful person and I start each day in a positive way.

BARBARA "WILLOW" DRINKWATER

Retired Realtor

After putting on my purple bracelet declaring I was part of the twenty-one-day Complaint Free challenge, I found my life positively changing.

People noticed and the extra bracelets in my purse were soon on my friends' wrists as they took the challenge. This made my environment happier! My daughter gave this all a fresh perspective when she said, "There are no problems, just things to do!"

One day my husband was so upset about something said at the dinner table that he stood up and walked out of the room. I don't even remember what was said, but within a minute, he came back, sat down, and said, referring to himself, "I don't know who that fella was I met in the hallway, but aren't you glad he's gone!" The Complaint Free concept was rubbing off on him, too.

I now catch myself before complaining and my mind switches away from problems to finding solutions. The Complaint Free challenge has taught me to be grateful and that, to use nautical terms, I am the skipper of my skiff!

DANIEL RIZZI

Chocolate Store Owner

I got to know Will Bowen's work back in 2016 when my wife, Eliana, sent me an article about the benefits of not complaining she found on a website here in Brazil. At that time, I complained a lot, which affected everyone around me, including my young son Pedro. The web article referred to Will's book *A Complaint Free World,* which was available in Portuguese.

I bought the book and learned how to develop the habit of being Complaint Free by going twenty-one days without complaining. Will explains that there are four stages to mastery: Unconscious Incompetence, Conscious Incompetence, Conscious Competence, and Unconscious Competence, and, believe me, I went through all the stages!

The process is simple: Put a Complaint Free bracelet on your wrist and every time you complain, change the bracelet to the other wrist and start over again back on Day 1.

I ordered the bracelets and started the twenty-one-day process without complaining. It took me two years, two months, and eight days of switching my bracelet before I completed the twenty-one days Complaint Free. Will Bowen sent me a Certificate of Happiness, which I proudly display on my desk to this day.

The secret is to never give up. I have since joined Will's Complaint Free Life Inner Circle. As a member, you post on Facebook what day you are without complaining to inspire yourself and other people! When we do not complain, we seek solutions in a very mature way without playing the role of victims. And that transformed every area of my life.

I continue to do the challenge every day and have completed the twenty-one days Complaint Free several times. As a result, I am more focused, my business has prospered, and my relationships with my employees and my family have greatly improved. Most importantly, I have started to like and take care of myself more! I'm even realizing my lifelong dream of becoming an officer with the São Paulo police department!

I believe that not complaining is synonymous with freedom, success, and wealth. But it is still a daily exercise of constant vigilance. In addition to not complaining, today I always watch myself not to gossip or say bad things about others.

I also learned from Will Bowen that by not complaining, we gradually deplete our brain's supply of negative thoughts, as it only supplies these negative thoughts as we verbalize them.

Staying with the twenty-one days of not complaining is addictive and I never want to stop. It is a great honor for me to be part of this experience! I feel very fulfilled and happy. I've learned that being happy is a matter of choice. It does not depend on external factors. You just choose to be happy. And I always want to be happy.

JEFF LENHART

In 2012, as part of a management team for a local company in my town, I was introduced to the book *A Complaint Free World*. All of our management team was required to read the book and try the Complaint Free challenge for at least thirty days.

This all came at a perfect time because I was struggling in my role from both the negativity of my co-workers and also myself. I quickly realized how much I complain during an average day even without realizing I was doing it!

I began to focus on myself and the complaints I would speak throughout my days, especially at work.

The following Christmas, Will Bowen created a contest on his Facebook page offering to come and speak in your community for free if your entry was selected. At that time, I was working for a different company but there was still a lot of negativity. So, I emailed Will, explaining how my city of Dubuque, Iowa, would benefit if he came here to speak to us.

Much to my surprise, Will emailed me two days later stating that I had won! I quickly formed a "Complaint Free" committee, to get community leaders involved in Will's trip to town, and also to let everyone know about the Complaint Free challenge.

Schools got involved, as well as other businesses and organizations, and even the local city council proclaimed a special "Complaint-Free Day"!

It's been ten years since Will came here to speak and people still talk about it, telling me how much they were inspired by reading *A Complaint Free World* and doing the purple bracelet challenge!

BRIAN MATTHYS

Dermatologist, Inventor, Author of *Dermboy Saves Vacation*

As a physician, I entered into a profession to help people. But interestingly, in medical jargon, a patient's concern is considered a "chief complaint." This is used in assessing the primary reason a person would see a doctor and come into the office.

So, Will's book may seem to fly in contrast to my profession. But his voice in my head helped change my practice, my profession, and my life. I bought everyone on my staff a copy of *A Complaint Free World* and we incorporated his techniques and his Complaint Free bracelets to help us change our mental story. A way to help us see that rather than complaining or gossiping, we should take action.

Complaints and worry don't improve a person's reality. Action does. Now, our staff (medical assistants, nurses, physicians, and admin team) looks at their words and listens to themselves in a whole new way.

Thank you to Will Bowen and the Complaint Free movement. We are so grateful that his words followed by our actions made a difference to both us and to our patients.

MIKE FINKELSTEIN

Executive Director of the Global Sports
Business Master's Degree Program, Rutgers University

When you think of someone in the field of sports management, your mind might conjure up a person who is hard-driving, success driven, and perhaps a little pushy. Maybe you find yourself visualizing Dwayne Johnson in *Ballers* or Tom Cruise in *Jerry Maguire*. People who are driven by money, power, and prestige.

When I began the sports management program at Rutgers, I knew that what was needed was a focus on what many people call "soft skills," including the ability to work well with others and, most importantly, a talent for remaining positive and upbeat during the many struggles and hard times that go with this profession.

In 2010, I read Will Bowen's book *A Complaint Free World* and I took the twenty-one-day challenge myself. What an eye-opener! I knew this would have to be part of the curriculum for these aspiring sports management professionals.

So, every Christmas break I give all of my students a copy of Will's book and instruct them to take the twenty-one-day Complaint Free challenge. Toward the end of the following term, each of them writes a paper on their experience, and their comments have reinforced my decision to make this a required part of the class each year.

Here are some sample comments from a handful of my students:

I will be up-front about my history of complaining. I have been consistently negative for years, and I never thought I would find a way to overcome it. I would complain about every aspect of my life. In sports I'd complain, "I am not on a good team, time to move somewhere else." In school, I'd complain, "How am I ever going to graduate? I am just not smart enough."

All these negative thoughts and complaints have damaged past relationships and made me question my abilities over and over. I never thought it would end.

That was until I read A Complaint Free World *by Will Bowen. What a coincidence that when I decided to make a significant life change by attending graduate school, I would also read the first book that would help put me on a positive path for the rest of my life.*

—ROSS BARON

What you gave us at the end of last semester is more than just a book. I look at it more like a life guide and something to live by.

A young adult just starting their life or someone who has already retired can both read this book and take away the same message. If you can master the twenty-one-day challenge and stop complaining, your world will become a better place in which to live.

—BRANDON LOREE

When my dad was diagnosed with terminal cancer, it completely uprooted my family and gave us a sobering wake-up call to shift our perspective to what we value and what we should prioritize. By reminding myself to control what I can, it helps me remember that I cannot dictate how others perceive me, but rather I can only have a say in my own reactions and feelings.

—JAIME MOSCHETTO

The benefits of being Complaint Free are the main motivator to keep working toward this lifestyle. Will's concept that "If venting our anger made us happier, then wouldn't the biggest complainers also be the happiest people?" made me consider the many benefits of not complaining and how they align with my life's goals.

My goal is to be happy. Complaining brings no solutions, but instead creates a snowball of emotions that will be insignificant in a week and nonexistent in a month.

In a short time, I have cleared up mental space and now have a more positive perspective. My hope is that, like Mr. Bowen, my life will be surrounded with individuals that also feel happier and Complaint Free. This challenge has not been easy and has required a lot of restraint, but I am glad I am pushing myself to make a positive impact on my life.

—CINDY RODRIGUEZ

As humans, we notice the complaints of others a lot more than we do our own. After reading the book, the complaints of others may begin to stick out even more than before, and so did my own.

Through my progress toward twenty-one Complaint Free days, I am developing the ability to catch a complaint before I let it out, which is helping me to channel that negative energy in a different way. I've found it to be extremely rewarding to be able to compartmentalize complaints and rephrase my feelings in an improved way. Among the four stages that Will outlines, I believe I currently am entering the Conscious Competence stage, where I am showing patience and being more careful when I speak.

—RYAN ROSE

A Complaint Free World *gives lessons on how to remain objective and helps us understand the root reasons as to why we complain, all the while encouraging readers to become more mindful of the power that words and thoughts have over our lives. Embarking on this journey has taught me many lessons, and the biggest one so far is that I need to get out of my own way. Additionally, this book has taught me why we complain as well as why we shouldn't complain, and it has urged me to create a personal action plan in my pursuit of becoming more mindful of my energy and the power that I possess.*

As a professor, I'm so grateful that my incorporating Will's book and the Complaint Free challenge into my course has so consistently had a positive impact on my students. This will continue to be an important part of my curriculum going forward.

—KRYSTAL WHITEHEAD

LIA MURPHY

A Complaint Free World Business Manager

My husband and I were on vacation in Hawaii a while ago and one night he and I went out for a walk. We strolled along the streets hand in hand talking about our lives and what we love most about each other. When I asked him what he loved about me, he responded, "Your unwavering positivity.

"I don't think you realize how positive you really are," he continued. "No matter what, you look for what is going well. If our air conditioner goes out and we don't have the money to pay for it, you say, 'At least we have an option to finance.' When one of our flights was canceled, you said, 'At least we are here together.'

"It's not that you don't get upset, you do," he said, squeezing my hand. "But you don't take things personally and you always find something to be happy about."

I guess this makes sense because my dad is Will Bowen and he introduced the Complaint Free challenge at our church in 2007 when I was only nine years old.

Despite the towers of boxes of bracelets stacked floor to ceiling in the church fellowship hall, I didn't fully understand the scope of the movement. I just knew it was a great jungle gym of boxes to play on for a bored kid who went to work with her dad during the summer. I first realized how big the movement was when my middle school class abandoned our lessons to watch The Oprah Winfrey Show to see if we could catch a glimpse of me sitting in the front row as my dad was interviewed.

Unlike the many other wonderful stories here, I didn't find the Complaint Free movement one day and it suddenly transformed my life. The Complaint Free movement molded me from a very young age into the person I am today.

Because of this I find myself having a hard time writing about all the ways that my life is better being Complaint Free, because I have nothing else to compare it to. This has simply been a part of my life for as long as I can remember.

But as an adult I began to see those around me were having a much harder time with life than I was. It seems that everything goes wrong for them all the time. They never seem to be happy or fulfilled in anything. Even a vacation to a perfect tropical paradise can be laden with turmoil, but that doesn't happen for me.

When I take a step back, I realize that my life is the same as theirs. I experience hardships, frustrations, and difficulties. They just don't hold the same weight for me as they do for most people. Something going wrong for me is only a hiccup and I will usually find something to be grateful for. I don't take the bad things that happen in my life personally and don't believe that the world is out to get me as some people do.

The joy and peace I feel from being a Complaint Free person is immeasurable, and though it doesn't mean that I am without frustration, occasional anxiety, or difficulties, I am far better equipped to handle whatever comes my way.

I truly believe that someone can forever change their life by choosing to be Complaint Free. The life you are currently living can feel easier, your relationships deeper and more meaningful, and you can find something to be grateful for even in the most difficult situations.

It's all up to you.

CONCLUSION

UVA UVAM VIDENDO VARIA FIT

—SIGN IN FRONT OF THE HAT
CREEK CATTLE COMPANY IN
LARRY MCMURTRY'S *LONESOME DOVE*

*How many a man has dated a
new era in his life from the reading of a book.*

—HENRY DAVID THOREAU

You have entered into a new era in your life.

The concepts you have learned in this book have tweaked your consciousness and opened up new possibilities whether you fully realize it or not. Chances are you have not even begun to embrace all the many ways your life will improve as a result of this process.

If you have spent your life focusing on clouds, soon you will begin to see the sunlight that brightly shines behind them. If you have been plagued by dissatisfaction, you will begin to find peace and joy. If you have seen only problems, you will begin to discover new possibilities. If your relationships have been discordant, you will begin to experience harmony.

You have planted a seed. It may seem to be just a small acorn, but in time it will grow into a majestic oak.

Your life is transforming.

Let me say one more time that you can succeed at becoming Complaint Free if you will just stay with it. People are creatures of habit. It takes time to replace old habits with new ones. But a habit is created with daily actions, like single brushstrokes on what will one day become a beautiful painting.

When I was a child, one of my favorite books my mother would read to me was about a baker, a miserly shopkeeper, and a mysterious stranger who enters their village. In this story, the stranger approaches the townsfolk seeking food and shelter for the night. When he asks the miserly shopkeeper and his wife if they will help him, the couple dismissively refuses to provide assistance.

The stranger then walks into the town's only bakery. The baker is penniless and nearly out of baking supplies. Nonetheless, he invites the man in and shares a meager meal with him. Next, the baker offers the weary traveler his own austere bed in which to sleep. The following morning the stranger awakens, thanks the baker, and tells him, "Whatever you do first this morning, that you will continue to do all day."

The baker is unsure as to the meaning of the stranger's comment and gives it little thought. He decides to bake his guest a cake to take with him. Surveying the last of his supplies, he finds two eggs, a cup of flour, a little sugar, and some spices. He begins to make the cake and discovers, much to his

surprise, that the more supplies he uses, the more he
has. As he draws out the last
two eggs, he notices four
more in their place. When

"We are what we repeatedly do.
Excellence, then, is not an act but
a habit."

—WILL DURANT

he tips the sack to shake out the last handful of flour, the sack
is full when he sets it down. Overjoyed with his good fortune,
the baker throws himself into baking all manner of delicacies,
and soon the town square is filled with the delicious aroma
of baked breads, cookies, cakes, and pies. Customers line up
around the block to purchase his confections.

That evening, tired, happy, and his cash register overflow-
ing, the baker is approached by the miserly shopkeeper. "How
did you get so many customers today?" the shopkeeper demands. "It looked like everyone in town bought baked goods
from you, some more than once." The baker shares the story of
the stranger he helped as well as the man's enigmatic blessing
prior to departing.

The shopkeeper and his wife run out of the bakery and
down the road leading away from town, searching for the
mysterious traveler. At last they find the very man they refused to help the previous evening. "Gentle sir," they say, "forgive our rudeness last night. We must have been out of our
heads not to help you. Please, return with us to our home and
allow us the honor of sharing our hospitality with you." Without a word, the man turns around and joins the couple on the
road back into town.

When they arrive at the shopkeeper's home, the traveler is fed a sumptuous meal accompanied with fine wine and a decadent dessert. The stranger is then offered a luxurious room for the night with a bed made from thick, cozy goose down.

The following morning as the visitor prepares to leave, the shopkeeper and his wife bounce up and down on their toes expectantly, waiting for him to cast his magic spell over them. Sure enough, the stranger thanks his hosts and says, "Whatever you do first this morning, that you will continue to do all day."

Having received the blessing, the shopkeeper's wife rushes the stranger out the door. She and her husband put on their cloaks and dash to their store. Expecting a large number of customers, the shopkeeper grabs a broom and begins to sweep the floor in preparation for the onslaught of traffic. Wanting to make sure they have enough change for the purchases certain to happen that day, his wife begins to count the money in the till.

The shopkeeper swept and his wife counted. She counted and he swept. Try as they might, they could not stop sweeping and counting until the day was over. When someone did enter their store, they were so compelled to continue sweeping and counting that they were unable to stop to sell anything.

Both the baker and the shopkeeper had received the same blessing. The baker began his day in a positive and generous way and received great reward. The shopkeeper began his day in a negative and self-serving way and derived nothing. The blessing was neutral.

Your ability to create your life is neutral. Use it

"The pessimist complains about the wind. The optimist expects it to change. The realist adjusts the sail."

—WILLIAM A. WARD

however you wish; you will reap what you sow. This story reminds us that when we do things for others out of compassionate generosity rather than selfishness, we experience great rewards.

An important secondary moral to this tale is to begin each day as we wish the remainder of the day to unfold. If you have not been able to go even one full day without complaining, see how long you *can* go without complaining after rising in the morning. If you will attempt to go just a little longer each morning without speaking that first complaint, you will find yourself progressing much more quickly and easily toward your twenty-one-day Complaint Free goal.

There is a term in computer programming usually expressed as an acronym: GIGO, which means "Garbage in, garbage out." If a computer does not perform properly, it is generally because there is something that has been input into the computer that is problematic. The garbage going in has generated garbage coming out. The computer is neutral.

Your life is like a computer—neutral. However, rather than "Garbage in, garbage out," you will experience "Garbage out, garbage in." When you speak, you send out vibrations and call more of what you say back to you. When you complain, you are sending out garbage and should, therefore, not be surprised when garbage shows up on your doorstep. Garbage out of your mouth means garbage in your life!

What you articulate, you demonstrate. Talk about negative and unhappy experiences, and you will receive more negative and unhappy experiences to talk about. Talk about things you appreciate, and you will draw more positive things to you. You have a habitual pattern of speaking that demonstrates what you are thinking, and this is creating your reality. Whether you realize it or not, you plot your course each day and then follow that course.

If you want to improve the world, it must first come from healing the discord within your own soul. Changing your words will ultimately change your thoughts, and this will, in turn, change the world. When you cease complaining, you remove the outlet for your negative thoughts, your mind shifts, and you become happier.

Once you complete twenty-one consecutive days Complaint Free, you will move from being a person who is addicted to complaining, to being one who is in recovery from a complaining addiction.

The Complaint Free challenge is a lot like the Alcoholics Anonymous program. Prior to when Bill W. and Dr. Bob created AA, many who suffered from the disease of alcohol addiction sought to curb their drinking through religion and psychiatry. AA, on the other hand, teaches that you should first stop drinking and then your life will heal. Similarly, don't wait for your life to improve to stop complaining. Stop complaining and your life will improve.

"The condition upon which God hath given liberty to man is eternal vigilance."

— JOHN PHILPOT CURRAN

Recovering alcoholics say that no matter how long they've been sober, if they spend enough time around booze, they're going to drink. If people around you are complaining, remain vigilant not to join in. You may even have to extricate yourself from negative relationships. If they are at your place of work, change departments or change jobs—the Universe will support you along your positive new path. If your friends chronically complain, you may realize that you have evolved beyond those present relationships and it's time to find new friends. Even if the negative relationships are with family members, it may be best to limit your time with those people.

Don't allow people who are negative to rob you of the life you desire. It takes twenty-one days to form a habit. You can reverse the Complaint Free habit with twenty-one days of your old behavior, so be wary of people around you, because you may be tempted to follow their lead. Take care of yourself and beware toxic, complaining people. If you are not mindful, you could be entrained by them and sink back into the mire of negativity.

Because of you and the tens of millions of people around the world who are, right now, switching their bracelets and continuing along the Complaint Free path, I have hope that the prevailing attitude of our world will shift.

I shared this hope with someone the other day who responded, "Sounds like false hope to me."

False hope? Let me share a story about "false hope."

It began at 1:10 A.M. on July 11, 2001. I was sound asleep, so it took several minutes for me to realize that the phone by my bed was ringing. Fumbling the receiver as I brought it to my ear, I croaked out a weak "Hello?"

"Will? It's Dave," my younger brother said. "Mom has had a heart attack and it doesn't look good. You better come, quick."

I got out of bed, packed a suitcase, and drove forty miles to the Kansas City airport. I tried to nap on the plane but found I was too worried. When my plane landed in Columbia, South Carolina, Dave picked me up.

As we drove to the hospital, Dave filled in the details. "Last night at about eight-thirty, she began to experience pain in her chest and back," he said. "She took some over-the-counter pain medications, but it didn't help. They took her to the hospital, but when they realized she was having a severe heart attack, the doctors had her flown via helicopter to the hospital that specializes in heart problems here in Columbia. She's awake but in a lot of pain."

Fifteen minutes later, Dave and I entered the Cardiac Critical Care Unit and found the room where our mother was sitting up with the aid of our oldest brother, Chuck. She was alert but was gasping slowly for breath. The medical staff gave us a few moments with her and then asked us to leave so she could rest.

Our mother fell into a deep sleep and didn't wake up. Echocardiograms showed that she had suffered a

"When one door of happiness closes, another opens; but often we look so long at the closed door that we do not see the one which has opened for us."

—HELEN KELLER

major heart attack. "It's as if a large portion of her heart has been blown out," said one doctor.

In case she regained consciousness, I chose to spend several of the subsequent nights sleeping in the waiting room. Many times each night I would go in and check on her, but she remained comatose, her breathing only possible thanks to a ventilator.

Even if you have no medical training, when you spend enough time with someone who is hooked up to a monitor that updates and reports vital signs, you can begin to discern when certain indicators are improving. Early one morning I noticed that my mom's blood oxygen level was rising and enthusiastically expressed this to her nurse.

"Don't get false hope," the nurse said with a doleful smile.

That afternoon, I left to take a shower and change my clothes. When I returned to the hospital, I ran into an old college fraternity brother who was then a senior cardiologist at this hospital. I asked him to review my mother's charts and tell me, honestly, her prognosis.

I returned with a cup of coffee an hour later to find my friend sitting in the waiting area, his face grim.

"It's not good," he said, shaking his head. "Her heart has suffered major damage. I know you don't want to hear this, but it seems that the machines are the only thing keeping her alive."

I slumped in a chair next to him as he placed a caring hand on my shoulder. As tears slipped down my cheeks, I stammered questions. "But can't *anything* be done? What about her vital signs? Some of them seem to be improving. Isn't that good? Doesn't that mean that she might recover?"

He squeezed my shoulder, took a deep breath, and said, "Will, yes, *some* of her vitals have improved—slightly—but it doesn't change the fact that she has suffered a major heart attack. A little improvement just isn't enough."

My friend let his words sink in and then said, "Earlier you asked me what I thought her chances of recovery were." He paused a moment before he continued, "Having reviewed her chart, I'd say only about fifteen percent."

"Okay," I said. "But that's fifteen percent, which is better than nothing, right?"

His compassionate gaze became stern. "Will, holding on to false hope is only going to make it more painful when she doesn't recover. I know you don't want to, but you have to face facts."

I tried to thank him, but I had no words. We exchanged a brief hug and he went back to his duties. I sat quietly and began to grieve my mother's passing.

That night, I lay on the floor of the waiting room unable to sleep as I remembered the wonderful times I had enjoyed with my mom. I thought of all the things yet to come that she would not get to see in the lives of her grandchildren. I thought of all the things yet unsaid. My soul felt like a

"Hope lies in dreams, in imagination, and in the courage of those who dare to make dreams into reality."

—JONAS SALK

chalkboard that had been raked by the fingernails of her sudden illness.

I padded in sock feet down to my mother's room to check on her. The repeated *shhhrrrr . . . fuhhhh* sound of the ventilator gave the room an industrial feeling. I sat in the chair next to Mom's bed and held her hand. As I gazed at the monitor, I saw that many, not just some but most, of her vital signs had improved from earlier that day. I pointed this out to the nurse who came in to change the bag of glucose that dripped into my mother's veins.

Looking up at the monitor, the nurse said, "Her stats are better." She then added, "But don't get false hope."

A shudder of anger came over me. I dropped my mother's hand, turned, and jogged briskly down the hallway back to the waiting room. Turning on the lights, I tore a page from my journal. I found a pen and began to write in large letters on the page. Again and again I retraced my pen strokes in an effort to make the letters as bold as possible. I then walked back to my mother's room and, using a piece of medical tape, pasted a sign on her monitor that read, THERE IS NO SUCH THING AS FALSE HOPE!

The word *hope* is defined as "a wish coupled with a

confident expectation of its fulfillment." So long as you hold a confident expectation that what you desire will come to pass, it can never be false.

False hope is an oxymoron.

My mother did pass away. But not for another ten years *after* that heart attack. She lived another decade in relatively good health. New arteries actually grew around the damaged areas of her heart, returning her blood flow to near-normal levels. My family and I had held a wish that she would recover coupled with a confident expectation of her doing so, and there is nothing more powerful.

Join me in the very real hope that humanity will continue to shift away from fear and negativity toward faith and optimism. Your becoming a Complaint Free person is the most important step toward that hope's becoming fulfilled. As one person changes, that person affects a great many people. Your thoughts, your actions, and especially your words ripple out to others and impact others—never forget that.

In Larry McMurtry's novel *Lonesome Dove,* a pseudointellectual cowboy named Gus McCrae carves a Latin motto into the bottom of a wooden sign he created for his livery business. The motto reads, UVA UVAM VIVENDO VARIA FIT.

McMurtry does not explain the motto and actually misspells it, I presume as a way of showing the cowboy's poor grasp of Latin. The correct spelling is *Uva Uvam Videndo Varia Fit,* which translates to "One grape changes color when it sees another." Put another way: One grape ripens another.

In a vineyard, one grape will begin to ripen, and in so doing it will send out a vibration, an enzyme, a fragrance, or an energy field of some kind, which is then picked up by the other grapes. This one grape signals the other grapes that it is time to change; it is time for them all to ripen. As you become a person who speaks only the highest for yourself and others, you will signal to everyone that it is time for a change. Without even trying, you will raise the consciousness of those around you. They will be entrained by you and begin to focus on what's going well rather than what's going wrong.

> "You cannot swim for new horizons until you have courage to lose sight of the shore."
> — WILLIAM FAULKNER

Entrainment is a powerful principle. I think this is why human beings like to hug one another. When we hug, even for just a brief second, one heart entrains with the other and we remind ourselves that there is only one life on this planet, a life we all share.

If we don't choose how we live our version of this one life with intention, we will live it by default, following along with others. Rather than knowing that we lead the flock, we will allow the flock to lead us. Human beings are herd animals. We follow others without even realizing we're doing so.

When my father was a young man, he managed a small motel owned by my grandfather. The motel was located directly across the street from a used car lot, and my dad worked out an arrangement with the owner of the car dealership. On evenings when the business was slow, my father was allowed to go over and move a dozen or so cars from the used car lot and park them in front of the motel. In a very short time, the motel would fill up with paying customers. Be-

"One dog barks at something, the rest bark at him."

—CHINESE PROVERB

cause of the herd mentality all human beings share, passersby figured that if the motel parking lot was empty, the motel wasn't very good. But if the motel's parking lot was full, the travelers believed it must be a good place to stay for the night.

People follow other people. And you have now become a person who is leading the world toward peace, understanding, and abundance for all.

One night, back when I lived in Missouri, I was awakened around three A.M. by coyotes howling in our pasture. The howling began with one lone coyote pup and spread through-out the pack. In a very short time, even our two dogs picked up the howling. Soon our neighbors' dogs began to howl, and the howling crept up the valley in every direction as dogs on all sides joined in. After a while, I could hear dogs for miles in every direction howling. The coyotes had created a ripple and it was spreading. And it all began with just one small coy-ote pup.

Who you are creates an impact on your world. In the past, your impact may have been negative because of your propen-sity to complain. Now, however, you are modeling optimism and a better world for all. You are a positive ripple in the great ocean of humanity that spreads around the world.

RESOURCES

Take the Complaint Free Challenge

Get an official Complaint Free bracelet, nine Fast Start videos, and more for FREE (you just pay shipping and handling).

www.ComplaintFreeChallenge.com

Join the Complaint Free Life Inner Circle

Become a member of a community of positive people and get the knowledge, accountability, and support you need to become a Complaint Free person in record time!

www.ComplaintFreeLife.com

Become a Complaint Free Certified Trainer

Learn the art, business, and content of becoming a professional speaker spreading the Complaint Free message around the world.

www.ComplaintFreeTrainer.com

Complaint Free Life Coaching

Receive a FREE life coaching evaluation session to learn how you can remove the blocks to your happiness and success and start living the life of your dreams NOW!

www.ComplaintFreeCoaching.com

Bracelets in Bulk and Programs for Parents, Relationships, Businesses, Schools, Churches, and Much More

Check out our full line of Complaint Free tools and resources to improve every area of your life.

www.ComplaintFreeStore.com

ACKNOWLEDGMENTS

Thank you to Dr. Maya Angelou for her kindness, inspiration, and wisdom.

Thank you to Edwene Gaines, who first proposed the idea of inspiring people to break the complaining habit by going twenty-one days in a row without uttering a single complaint.

Thank you to Dr. Robin Kowalski, whose research has helped me contextualize Complaint Free living.

Thank you to Steve Hanselman of LevelFiveMedia, who has been my literary agent and friend for nearly two decades.

Thank you to the nearly forty publishers around the world who saw the promise in this book and brought it, in dozens of languages, to their countries.

Thank you to Penguin Random House for their continued faith and support.

And above all, thank you, dear reader, for being open to a new paradigm for your life and thereby helping to awaken our world.

ENDNOTES

1. M. E. Scheier, C. S. Carver, and M. W. Bridges, "Distinguishing Optimism from Neuroticism (and Trait Anxiety, Self-Mastery, and Self-Esteem): A Re-evaluation of the Life Orientation Test," *Journal of Personality and Social Psychology* 67 (1994): 1063–78.

Will Bowen is founder of the Complaint Free® movement with over 15 million followers worldwide. Will's been featured on *The Oprah Winfrey Show* and NBC's *Today* show, as well as in *People, Forbes, Newsweek, The Wall Street Journal,* and *Chicken Soup for the Soul*. Will Bowen is a top keynote speaker at conferences for businesses and associations worldwide, a #1 international bestselling author, and the world authority on complaining—why people complain, what's wrong with complaining, and how to get ourselves and others to stop complaining.

Learn more at WillBowen.com.